AF326568

Touching the Bones of Elisha

Touching *the* Bones *of* Elisha

Nine Life-Giving Spiritual Practices
from an Ancient Prophet

Albert Haase, O.F.M.

AND

Phil Vestal

FOREWORD BY
Christine Aroney-Sine

CASCADE *Books* · Eugene, Oregon

TOUCHING THE BONES OF ELISHA
Nine Life-Giving Spiritual Practices from an Ancient Prophet

Cascade Books
An Imprint of Wipf and Stock Publishers
199 W. 8th Ave., Suite 3
Eugene, OR 97401

www.wipfandstock.com

PAPERBACK ISBN: 978-1-6667-6073-6
HARDCOVER ISBN: 978-1-6667-6074-3
EBOOK ISBN: 978-1-6667-6075-0

Cataloguing-in-Publication data:

Names: Haase, Albert [author]. | Vestal, Phil [author]. | Aroney-Sine, Christine [foreword].

Title: Touching the bones of Elisha : nine life-giving spiritual practices from an ancient prophet / by Albert Haase and Phil Vestal ; foreword by Christine Aroney-Sine.

Description: Eugene, OR: Cascade Books, 2023 | Includes bibliographical references.

Identifiers: ISBN 978-1-6667-6073-6 (paperback) | ISBN 978-1-6667-6074-3 (hardcover) | ISBN 978-1-6667-6075-0 (ebook)

Subjects: LCSH: Elisha (Biblical prophet). | Prophets. | Bible.—Kings, 2nd—Criticism, interpretation, etc. | Spiritual life—Religious aspects—Christianity. | Bible.—Kings—Criticism, Narrative.

Classification: BS1335.2 H33 2023 (print) | BS1335.2 (ebook)

04/24/23

As soon as the [dead] man touched the bones of Elisha,
he came to life and stood on his feet. (2 Kgs 13:21)

Contents

Foreword

I AM A BIT of a rebel when it comes to spiritual practices. I don't like the accepted ways of praying without movement or reading the scriptures without encouragement to put the words I read into action. You can blame the time I spent in the refugee camps in Thailand for that. My experiences left me craving an embodied faith that was lived out in every aspect of my life.

When I came across the liturgical calendar some years later, Advent wreaths, stations of the cross, and other activities that encouraged the use of all our senses, seemed like a gift from heaven. Unfortunately, I soon got bored with the traditional ways to celebrate the liturgical seasons and found myself looking for something new. I started creating Advent and other meditation gardens. They began as a way to mark the seasons of the liturgical calendar, but slowly became a way of life, often inspired by the world events that pulled at my heartstrings with both joy and sorrow. More and more, they became a tool through which I listened to the promptings of the Holy Spirit both within me and in the world around me. Eventually these gardens resulted in me developing a process of dreaming, creating, meditating, and letting go as a template for new spiritual practices. This approach revolutionized my life as I applied it not only to the creation of gardens but to other practices for the celebration of events on the liturgical calendar and seasons in my life. It enriched and strengthened my faith and drew me closer to God in many unexpected ways.

The process I developed is all about paying attention. Paying attention as we wander and take notice of what is around us. Paying attention as we allow what we see to stir our imaginations and spark new ideas. Paying attention as we create practices to strengthen our spiritual lives and ground us more firmly in our faith. And paying attention as we let go of what we created and see that even in the putting to rest of an existing practice, new ideas and thoughts evolve into something fresh for a new season of our lives.

Part of what I loved as I read *Touching the Bones of Elisha,* was that Albert Haase and Phil Vestal display the same spirit of adventure and creativity when it comes to their understanding of spiritual practices. They pay attention to the life of Elisha, to the lessons they learn from each other, and to the needs of the world that pull at their heartstrings. It delights me to see them take Elisha—an often neglected, yet important prophet from the Old Testament—as their guide. They allow Elisha's voice to speak to them in unique ways, combining the principles of ancient spiritual practices with modern stories and perspectives that not only make the whole story of Elisha come to life, but also inspire us to incorporate new practices in our own spiritual journey.

The practices Phil and Albert talk about really resonate with me. Like them, I am a strong believer in the need to pay attention to the call of God and not allow distractions to divert my attention. I also know the importance of opening myself to God's healing for my past experiences and of standing firm when I face opposition. Like them, I know the incredible ways God provides for us when we let go of high-paying possibilities for the ways of faith. I struggle however to pray and then trust God and I am still learning to be sensitive to others, and to show mercy to my enemies, probably one of the greatest challenges all of us face.

I don't think that spiritual practices are meant to be static. Nor is prayer and scripture reading enough to sustain us. As we read the Bible and listen to the lives of those who went before us, we become aware that many of them, like Jesus, drew on the spirituality of their ancestors but transformed their practices in ways that touched the hearts of their followers. I suspect that one of Jesus' teachers was Elisha, and I imagine he would benefit from some of the same lessons that he learned. As we grow in our faith and expand our understanding of God, our ways of practicing our faith change. This book will, I believe, help all of us think in fresh ways and strengthen our relationship to God, to each other, and to the purposes God has for us.

Christine Aroney-Sine

Introduction

A Protestant minister and a Roman Catholic priest go to a bar to discuss an Old Testament prophet of Israel . . .

It sounds like the beginning of a joke, doesn't it? It's not exactly how the idea for this book came about—alcohol, however, was involved.

In the final months of 2019, Phil invited Albert to be a guest on his *Ruah Space* podcast to discuss Albert's recently published book, *Becoming an Ordinary Mystic: Spirituality for the Rest of Us.* We enjoyed each other's company. Because listeners commented on how interesting it was that a Protestant pastor and a Roman Catholic priest found common ground to discuss spiritual formation, Phil invited Albert to return on two more occasions. We discussed "Dryness, Desolation, Darkness, and Depression: Struggles on Our Faith Journey" and "Lectio Divina on Your Life." At the beginning of the 2020 pandemic, we filmed twelve twenty-minute segments called "An At-Home Retreat with the Lord's Prayer" that remain available on YouTube.

By this point, we were more than collaborators. Without either of us being consciously aware of it, a friendship had blossomed, though 1,100 miles separated us, and we had never met in person.

During a Zoom conversation—it didn't happen in a bar—Albert was sipping a glass of red wine in his Texas office while Phil sipped a beer on his porch in Florida.

"What about coauthoring a book?" Phil asked. "With our common knowledge of Scripture and your additional knowledge of the history of Christian spirituality, I think we could come up with something unique."

"What exactly would be the subject of the book?"

"How about the prophet Elisha and the spiritual practices derived from reflection on incidents in his life?" Phil asked.

Albert grimaced and was silent. *We Catholics know the four Gospels, but when it comes to the Old Testament, we're not the sharpest tacks on the bulletin board.*

"Why don't you read the Elisha stories in the First and Second Books of Kings? Reflect on them and then we can talk later," Phil suggested.

Albert breathed a sigh of relief that he didn't have to embarrass himself and ask where the Elisha stories were found. The Zoom call ended. After pouring a second glass of wine, Albert opened his Bible.

Two weeks later, Albert called Phil.

"I'm in. Let's do this! I think the Elisha cycle suggests some spiritual practices that are not only important, but also perennial. I've got energy around this idea. It's unique and could be a real blessing for readers. I have just one reservation."

"What's that?" Phil asked.

"I don't want it destroying our friendship."

"We're on the same page," Phil replied. "I thought the same thing. With fourteen books under your belt, you're the more experienced writer. I'll just have to trust your judgment about what works and doesn't work."

And with that, toasting virtually with a glass of red wine and a bottle of beer, the idea for *Touching the Bones of Elisha: Nine Life-Giving Spiritual Practices from an Ancient Prophet* was born.

Who was the man who is the subject of this book? Elisha (his name means "God is salvation" in Hebrew) was a prophet of the northern kingdom of Israel during the reigns of Joram, Jehu, Jehoahaz, and Jehoash (ca. 850–800 BC). A disciple of Elijah, he continued his master's prophetic mission with a double portion of Elijah's spirit after Elijah was lifted to heaven in a fiery chariot (2 Kgs 2:1–12). Unlike Elijah, who lived in caves in the desert, Elisha stayed in cities (2 Kgs 6:13, 19, 32) and maintained a home in Samaria (2 Kgs 2:25; 5:3; 6:32). He is often found in the company of groups of prophets ("the sons of the prophets"; 2 Kgs 2:3–15; 4:1; 5:22; 9:1). He was a man of wisdom and a worker of miracles on behalf of needy individuals and his nation.

We have chosen to reflect on ten events in the life of the prophet Elisha found in the First and Second Books of Kings:

- his response to God's prophetic call (1 Kgs 19:19–21);

- breaking Joshua's curse on the waters of Jericho (2 Kgs 2:19–22);

- the opposition he faced as he approached Bethel (2 Kgs 2:23–25);

- the multiplication of oil to help a prophet's widow importuned by a harsh creditor (2 Kgs 4:1–7) and the miracle of feeding a hundred people with twenty barley loaves and leaving leftovers (2 Kgs 4:42–44);

- his intercession for a Shunammite woman to give birth to a son—and then raising that deceased son from the dead (2 Kgs 4:8–37);

- the cure of leprous Naaman and the commander's response (2 Kgs 5:1–19);

- the miraculous repair and recovery of a borrowed, broken ax from the Jordan River (2 Kgs 6:1–7);

- thwarting an Aramean attack (2 Kgs 6:8–19);

- feeding the enemy (2 Kgs 6:20–23).

As we coauthored this book, we discovered together that this ancient prophet offers twenty-first-century believers nine spiritual practices and principles that anticipate and resonate with the teachings of Jesus, Saint Paul, and the subsequent history of Christian spirituality. We think of these practices as the life-giving bones left behind by Elisha (see 2 Kgs 13:21); hence, the title for this book.

As we discussed the stories about this prophet, we were reminded that dedication to God's call brooks no rivals and is all-consuming. We faced the reality that memories sometimes need to be healed. We discovered how to respond to opposition. We learned how to live in a whole new economic system based upon God's reign. We uncovered an important attitude about prayer. We were stretched by the way our freedom sometimes requires a unique form of obedience. We were awestruck by God's investment and protection in our lives. We were tested in how to treat an enemy.

Elisha's spiritual practices and principles are just as challenging today as they were thousands of years ago when Elisha first accepted God's call to become a prophet. The fact that they are continued in our Christian spiritual tradition speaks to their abiding attraction and enduring efficacy.

You will meet some people in these pages who are shining examples of individual Elisha practices. In the cases of those who are publicly known, their names and details have remained unchanged. In the cases of those personally known only to Phil or Albert, their names and details have been changed.

To foster a deeper appreciation for an individual Elisha practice, each chapter concludes with four simple elements: *Reflect* provides a question to consider. *Practice* highlights a spiritual technique or action to try. *Ponder* offers a quotation for reflection. *Pray* is a short prayer that captures the essence of the chapter's Elisha practice. These four elements provide an incentive for personal reflection or public discussion in a book study.

When it comes to the experience of God and spiritual formation, Christians of different denominations are more united than we might think. However, as we interpret our experiences and practices through the lens of our different denominational creeds with their unique theologies, divisions arise. We hope that *Touching the Bones of Elisha: Nine Life-Giving Spiritual Practices from an Ancient Prophet* will unite all believers in the practice of spiritual formation and be a contribution to fulfilling Jesus' dream "that they may all be one. As you, Father, are in me and I am in you, may they also be in us, so that the world may believe that you have sent me" (John 17:21).

We also hope this book encourages you to invite a friend from another faith tradition to share together a meal and a glass of wine while discussing the Bible and its impact on your spiritual formation. If anyone should raise an eyebrow, remember Jesus himself was accused of being "a glutton and a drunkard" (Matt 11:19).

Albert Haase, OFM, and **Phil Vestal**

Destroy the Farm
1 Kings 19:19–21

"Erin and I graduated from college in May 2010. We got married the following month, and in early July, we found ourselves in the back of a small pickup going to the village of Namwera, Malawi, near the border with Mozambique," Phil told Albert during a Zoom conversation.

"Wow! You're the only person I know who took his wife on an African safari for their honeymoon." Albert chuckled.

"Well, actually, I had nothing to do with it," Phil confessed.

"What do you mean?"

"It was *God's* idea!" Phil responded.

"What?"

"We felt called as a couple to do missionary activity. So during our senior year, we researched different Christian organizations where we could volunteer. None of them really grabbed us, so we gave up searching. Then in February, my mother phoned. 'Phil,' she said, 'I met the most interesting man who has started attending our church. He runs a Christian volunteer organization and is looking for a pastor and a teacher who would be willing to move to a farm and orphanage in Malawi and minister for the foreseeable future. There's just one catch—you have to raise your own funds. Anyway, as soon as I heard him say he's looking for two volunteers, I instantly thought of you and Erin.' She gave me the contact information.

"I couldn't wait to tell Erin. As we discussed it, lots of questions suddenly came to the surface. What would our family and friends think? Erin knows I'm really uncomfortable asking people for money. Would we be able to raise the funds needed? We each had a little bit of savings, but was it wise to spend it on such an adventure as this? And what about the master's program I was about to begin?

"Neither of us had answers to all the questions and concerns. All we had was a growing conviction that we had to respond.

"I contacted the organization to get more information. And that's when reality set in. We would have to give up chocolate chip cookies, the American way of doing things, and our Netflix subscription. When I asked about internet access, I was told that we would have to drive five hours, assuming the weather cooperated, to the city of Blantyre. I still remember waking up in the middle of the night and thinking, *I won't be able to play fantasy football.* I'm embarrassed to admit it, but I had to ask myself if that was a deal breaker. The more I thought and prayed about it, the more I realized it wasn't.

"What cinched the deal for both of us was, one night while we were praying, it dawned on us once again: *Where the grace of God calls us, the grace of God will keep us.* Before we knew it, we were bumping up and down on top of a pile of luggage in the back of that small pickup on our way to Namwera."

Albert listened with amazement and once again realized just how mysterious—and ordinary—the call of God can be.

Elijah

Scripture is filled with people who witness to the call of God and the challenges it often entails. Think of Elijah and Elisha.

Elijah appears out of nowhere in the First Book of Kings as a prophetic zealot of the Lord fighting against idolatry. He declared a drought to punish the Israelites for the worship of Ba'al. During this drought, he was forced to hide but miraculously survived (1 Kgs 17:1–7).

The drought ended in a contest between Yhwh and Ba'al: the true god would be revealed by sending fire from heaven.

Yhwh was vindicated and the prophets of Ba'al were slaughtered (1 Kgs 18:20–40).

This infuriated Queen Jezebel who sought vengeance for the prophets of Ba'al. Elijah fled to Horeb where he had some frank words for God: "I have been very zealous for the Lord, the God of hosts; for the Israelites have forsaken your covenant, thrown down your altars, and killed your prophets with the sword. I alone am left, and they are seeking my life, to take it away" (1 Kgs 19:14). He was lamenting the challenges, sacrifices, and dangers in remaining faithful to his prophetic call.

In response, Yhwh commissioned Elijah to anoint Hazael as king over Aram/Syria, Jehu as king over Israel, and "Elisha son of Shaphat of Abel-meholah as prophet in your place" (vv. 15–16).

How was this message communicated to Elijah? A direct face-to-face encounter? Was it a deep-seated feeling? A hankering of the heart? A decision based on previous experience that Hazael, Jehu, and Elisha were worthy and good people? A brooding idea that gradually rose to consciousness? A sudden flash of insight that raced across the mind like a shooting star? We are not told.

The Call of Elisha

All we are told is that Elijah immediately set out in search of Elisha. Unlike Phil and Erin's call, which began with a desire, was mediated through a new member of Phil's mother's church, and offered time to discuss, reflect, and pray over its consequences, Elisha's call came through the person of Elijah and it was abrupt.

The prophet found him in a field. Elisha "was plowing. There were twelve yoke of oxen ahead of him, and he was with the twelfth." The detail of twelve pairs of oxen suggests his father was a successful and wealthy landowner. "Elijah passed by him and threw his mantle over him" (v. 19). That action of covering Elisha with his cloak indicates the call to follow the prophet and serve him (v. 21). No doubt aware of the consequences, did Elisha accept the call?

Elisha responded immediately. "He left the oxen, ran after Elijah, and said, 'Let me kiss my father and my mother, and then I will follow you'" (v. 20).

Elijah approved his request but also used a question to remind the future prophet of the significance of the symbolic action: "Go back again; for what have I done to you?" (v. 20). Elijah wanted Elisha to ponder the question for himself. Did Elisha truly understand the significance, cost, and consequences of this call?

Diversions and Distractions

Elijah's question might have been a clarion call for Elisha to remember the call after he bid his parents farewell. Perhaps emotions circulating around the send-off and departure would pull at Elisha's heart and cause him to hesitate, waffle, or vacillate. Or maybe Elisha would second-guess his decision to follow Elijah after its consequences began to sink in and he realized he would no longer be earning a living by working the land. "For what have I done to you?" might have been a subtle reminder to stay focused and trusting despite emotional distractions, alluring diversions, and enticing interruptions.

Remember how Phil, a fantasy football fan, had to deliberately ask himself if giving up his team and not being able to watch sports were deal breakers? It wasn't just his football team he had to give up; it was also the community of friends he had made in the fantasy football league. The call of God always requires sacrifices.

The hair on the nape of his neck lifted when Phil saw the doctor bringing in a suitcase full of vaccines that he and Erin were going to need to stay healthy in Africa. The couple locked eyes and were tempted to revisit their decision after the doctor told them that Malawi was home to the highly dangerous, venomous black mamba snake, known to stand as tall as the couple and move even faster. Tongue in cheek, the doctor advised, "If you are bitten, find a comfortable tree to sit under so you can die in peace. It will take three hours at most." The couple failed to appreciate the doctor's humor.

Because God calls us to leave our comfort zones and trust in a journey to unknown lands and new experiences—sometimes across the continent and sometimes across the street—we might be tempted to dig in our heels and stay put. Or to delay until we have all our ducks in a row. We might straddle the fence and justify our hesitancy with cold logic and concerned logistics. We allow myriad voices to convince us to waffle and wait. We get sidetracked with distractions that are large and obvious—maybe health concerns—or small and insignificant—like internet access.

Elisha Destroys the Farm

Elijah's question, "For what have I done to you?" clearly reverberated in Elisha's soul and stirred him to action. He could have hired family or friends to work the land while he was away. He could have sold the oxen and plows to provide an income for his father. Instead, after bidding his parents farewell, he "took the yoke of oxen, and slaughtered them; using the equipment from the oxen, he boiled their flesh, and gave it to the people, and they ate. Then he set out and followed Elijah, and became his servant" (1 Kgs 19:21).

Elisha's decision to destroy the farm is significant. The farm could no longer divert his attention or distract him; it could no longer provide a plan B if the prophetic calling proved too challenging. It represented a bold break from the past, a clear commitment to the future, and the decisive determination in the present to serve God and Elijah.

Disciples of Jesus

Jesus himself combined a sense of urgency with this required break, commitment, and determination when approached by three would-be disciples.

> As they were going along the road, someone said to him, "I will follow you wherever you go." And Jesus

said to him, "Foxes have holes, and birds of the air have nests; but the Son of Man has nowhere to lay his head." To another he said, "Follow me." But he said, "Lord, first let me go and bury my father." But Jesus said to him, "Let the dead bury their own dead; but as for you, go and proclaim the kingdom of God." Another said, "I will follow you, Lord; but let me first say farewell to those at my home." Jesus said to him, "No one who puts a hand to the plow and looks back is fit for the kingdom of God." (Luke 9:57–62)

Jesus is not simply calling the first seeker to homelessness. He is, in effect, reminding the would-be disciple that personal comfort would have to give way to the demands of discipleship. Phil and Erin learned this firsthand in their call to Malawi.

He challenged the second inquirer to detach from conventional cultural obligations. Middle Eastern customs included the filial obligation for an elder son to honor his deceased father with a proper funeral before leaving the family household.[1] Conversely, discipleship meant committing to a life-giving relationship with Jesus. Those who refuse it are considered spiritually dead—and they can bury the physically dead.[2] According to Jesus, the proclamation of the kingdom of God supersedes all cultural duties, responsibilities, and obligations.

Was Jesus alluding to Elisha's call with the third would-be disciple? Using the agrarian image drawn from daily life, Jesus was making his point clearly and succinctly: a disciple cannot be walking forward as he guides his plow and looking backward to what was left behind. The kingdom not only requires concentration, focus, and a single-minded devotion; it also does not tolerate diversions, distractions, or disruptions.

Jesus was unrelenting and adamant on this point:

- Knowing well the pull of familial and cultural ties, he taught that whoever loves father, mother, son, or daughter more than him is not worthy to be his disciple (Matt 10:37).

1. Bailey, *Peasant Eyes*, 22–32.
2. Patella, "The Gospel according to Luke," 1,131.

- He emphasized the physical commitment of discipleship: neither hand, foot, nor eye can provide a diversion or distraction (Matt 5:29–30; 18:8–9).

- Intuiting how possessions had gripped the heart of the rich young man, Jesus encouraged him to sell his possessions, give the money to the poor, and then become his disciple (Matt 19:21).

- Knowing just how duplicitous the human heart can be, he stated, "No one can serve two masters; for a slave will either hate the one and love the other, or be devoted to the one and despise the other. You cannot serve God and wealth" (Matt 6:24).

These hard sayings of Jesus are rooted in hyperbole, a common teaching device used at the time of Jesus: They are not calling for hatred, self-mutilation, or absolute poverty. Rather, they are stinging reminders that when it comes to the things of God, no diversion, distraction, or disruption—however good, noble, or laudable—can be tolerated.

The Distraction of "Flies"

Saint Francis of Assisi often referred to distractions during prayer as "flies." His first biographer narrates an incident that occurred during the penitential season of Lent. In order not to idle away his time during those forty days, Francis spent his spare time making a small cup. One day, while praying, his attention gravitated toward the cup he was making. He became interiorly upset because he felt he was ignoring and insulting God by focusing on it.

"How could such a trifle have so much power over me as to bend my soul to itself?" he asked. "Since it sacrificed my time with God, I will sacrifice it to God."

He took the cup, threw it into the fire, and exclaimed, "We should be embarrassed when we are distracted by petty things."[3]

3. This is a paraphrase of a story found in Thomas of Celano, *The Remembrance of the Desire*, 311.

Nothing, Nothing, Nothing, Nothing, Nothing, Nothing

Like Elisha's, the young Francis's response to the distraction no doubt strikes the contemporary reader as rather severe. And in many ways, it was. But this kind of response continues to be a time-tested, common approach to spiritual formation.

A radical renunciation of all things, both physical and spiritual, is nowhere more evident than in the approach of the sixteenth-century Carmelite mystic Saint John of the Cross. He imagined the spiritual journey as an arduous hike up Mount Carmel. In a famous chart he drew of that journey,[4] he made it perfectly evident that the spiritual pilgrim must renounce not only the material things of the world, but also the very *desire* for spiritual gifts and experiences. Summing up what the pilgrim brings on the spiritual journey, John of the Cross writes in his native Spanish, "*Nada, nada, nada, nada, nada, nada*" ("Nothing, nothing, nothing, nothing, nothing, nothing"). Elisha and the young Francis of Assisi would nod approvingly.

Elisha, Jesus, Francis of Assisi, and John of the Cross each reminds us that hearing and responding to God's call require a heart free and unencumbered by distractions or diversions. Elisha witnesses to the occasional necessity of making a clean break from that which we might hold near and dear; this sometimes might have repercussions on our bank accounts. Jesus reveals that some cultural obligations and matters of the heart might hinder our commitment to discipleship; this might mean the renegotiation or even termination of some important relationships. The young Francis of Assisi reveals that even the smallest distraction can soften our decisive dedication to God; this could affect our hobbies and how we spend our time. And John of the Cross reminds us that even the *desire* for spiritual gifts and experiences can sabotage and hijack our response to the call of God; this suggests the spiritually mature are those who live with open hands.

4. Esparza, "The Mystical Drawings."

Inventory of the Heart

How do we grow in the freedom that captivated Elisha, Francis of Assisi, and John of the Cross? How can we be more attuned and ready to respond to the call of God? One practical way is to take an inventory of the heart to discover those chains of slavery and unfreedom that constrict us.

Spend twenty minutes in silence and solitude. Reflect on your childhood and subsequent history, your personality, your weaknesses and sins, and your commitment to God. Ponder the people and events that have been influential in your life and have provided security and comfort. Then write down the answers to the following questions:

Fears

What are the fears that grip my heart? What worries and concerns typically make me withhold an immediate response to God's invitation? What causes me apprehension, angst, and dread? Where do I feel imprisoned? In what dungeons do I feel confined?

How can I find the antidote of courage?

Attachments

What are the possessions, people, and opinions that weigh me down? That free me up? What are the heavy burdens that I choose to cling to and refuse to put in the hands of God? To whom and to what am I wholeheartedly devoted? Finish this sentence. "I cannot see myself living without . . ."

How can I learn to live with detachment and open hands?

Control Issues

What areas of my life cause me frustration and require that I take constant control? How do I dodge and avoid the feeling of helplessness? Over what do I insist having power and authority?

What practices help me to go through life with trust?

Sense of Entitlement

When do I hear myself saying, "I deserve this"? Over what do I claim rightful ownership? How does a feeling of privilege influence my thoughts, words, and actions? In what areas of my life do I insist on getting my own way?

How can I grow in humility?

This inventory reveals the heart's "face"—fears, attachments, control issues, and entitlements. It discloses where we have shut the door to God's invitation and call. Knowing those places in which fears, attachments, the need to be in control, and a sense of entitlement dominate our lives are critical in spiritual formation, as God attempts to upend our lives in those very places. Courage, detachment, trust, and humility are timeless remedies to the distractions and diversions that hinder our response to God.

"Contemplatives in Action"

Listening and responding to this call of God plays a major role in the spirituality of Saint Ignatius of Loyola, the sixteenth-century founder of the Society of Jesus, commonly called the Jesuits. Ignatian spirituality is premised on the idea that each of us is called by God to be a coworker with Jesus in promoting the kingdom of God. Consequently, like Elisha, a person actively detaches him- or herself from personal hindrances, obstacles, and impediments to that task. In doing so, they become free to discover and respond. A special prayer technique designed by Ignatius, called the Examen, invites a person to reflect on the ordinary experiences of his or her day with one question in mind: what was God asking of me in today's events and circumstances? One of Ignatius's first followers, a Spaniard named Jerome Nadal, coined the Ignatian expression, "contemplatives in action," referring to people who are constantly listening and responding to God's daily invitations and calls.

In the spirit of Elisha and Ignatius of Loyola, we are called to listen to God's active requests in the nitty-gritty of our daily experience. Nothing must distract or divert our attention from that call. The inventory of the heart reveals those areas where we are shackled and thus unable to freely respond. Upon discovery of our distractions and diversions, we are challenged to follow the example of Elisha and "destroy the farm."

Reflect

What are the "pots" and "farms" in my life that need to be destroyed? How do I feel about that? What issues, worries, or concerns are raised when I think of getting rid of them?

Practice

Take the inventory of the heart described in this chapter. After taking it, note where you have shut the door of your heart to God's invitation and call.

Ponder

> It makes little difference whether a bird is tied by a thin thread or by a cord. Even if it is tied by thread, the bird will be held bound just as surely as if it were tied by cord; that is, it will be impeded from flying as long as it does not break the thread. Admittedly the thread is easier to break, but no matter how easily this may be done, the bird will not fly away without first doing so. This is the lot of those who are attached to something: No matter how much virtue they have they will not reach the freedom of the divine union.
>
> —Saint John of the Cross[5]

Pray

Loving God, you call me to be a coworker with Jesus in promoting your kingdom. But fears, attachments, control issues, and a sense of entitlement weigh me down and impede my free and spontaneous response. Give me Elisha's courage, detachment, trust, and humility so that I might enthusiastically welcome and immediately respond to your daily invitations. In Jesus' name, I pray. Amen.

5. St. John of the Cross, *The Ascent*, Book One, 11.4, 143.

Break from the Past

2 Kings 2:19–22

ON OCTOBER 6, 1945, William Sianis, a Greek immigrant and owner of the Billy Goat Tavern, took his goat named Murphy to Wrigley Field in Chicago for game 4 of the World Series between the Detroit Tigers and Chicago Cubs. Cub fans were excited as they filed into the stadium on that fall afternoon; their team was up two games to one in the series. A win that day would give them a formidable lead in the seven-game battle.

At some point during the game, Wrigley Field officials approached Sianis and told him to leave the stadium because Murphy was bothering too many fans. Incensed, Mr. Sianis declared, "Them Cubs, they ain't gonna win no more."

He was correct: the Cubs lost that game, the next game, and the seventh game in the series. The championship drought, started in 1908, continued.

By Zoom, Phil was telling Albert this story. "It's called the 'curse of the billy goat,'" he continued, making quotation marks in the air by curling his index and middle fingers. "And it would stick to the Cubs for seventy-one years."

"I get it," Albert said. "I was born and raised in New Orleans, the voodoo capital of the world. I know all about the power of a curse, a spell, a hex, and the jinx. If you don't know the secret to breaking them, they can linger for a long time."

"You don't really believe in the power of a curse, do you?" Phil asked. "If you do, you are like a lot of other superstitious people who tried to break the curse of the billy goat. Sianis's nephew,

Sam, went to Wrigley Field with a goat multiple times in attempts to break the curse, including on Opening Day in 1984 and again in 1989. In 2007, a butchered goat was hung from the statue of Harry Caray, the famed Cubs' broadcaster for sixteen years, leading one newspaper reporter to note, 'If the prankster intended to reverse the supposed billy goat curse with the stunt, it doesn't appear to have worked.'[1] The following year, a Greek Orthodox priest unsuccessfully attempted to break the curse by sprinkling holy water in and around the Cubs' dugout. And probably the most creative attempt that also failed was started by Jeremy Freeman in 2011. He began Reverse the Curse, a fun campaign originally focused on the Cubs that morphed into lifting the curse of poverty and hunger in Chicago, the Dominican Republic, and Haiti, by giving people dairy goats and technical training to start their own business. There were at least eight other attempts to break the curse, but they all failed."

"Like I said, Phil, I know all about the power of a curse, a spell, a hex, and the jinx," Albert knowingly smiled.

"You'll be surprised to know how the curse was broken. It had nothing to do with superstitious incantations or sacrificed goats. In 2009, Tom Ricketts and his family reached an agreement with the Tribune Company to purchase the Cubs, Wrigley Field, and the regional Comcast SportsNet Chicago for close to $900 million. Over the next seven years, Ricketts overhauled the entire organization from the general manager to the players. That family chose to believe that they didn't have to live under the curse, that belief in the curse was a self-fulfilling prophecy. And guess what? In front of more than 38,000 fans, the curse of the billy goat was broken the night of November 2, 2016, in a game one reporter called 'the greatest World Series Game 7 ever.'[2] At the end of the ninth inning, the Cubs were tied with the Cleveland Indians 6–6. A sudden cloudburst caused a seventeen-minute rain delay. During the delay, some believed the curse was rearing its ugly head again and the rain would wash away yet another shot at victory. Instead, during the

1. Toomey, "Dead Goat," *Chicago Sun-Times*.
2. Armour, "Why Cubs, Indians," *USA Today Sports*.

delay, Cubs right fielder Jason Heyward reminded his teammates that they were the best team in baseball and had to stick together to win. And as the old saying goes, 'The rest is history.'

"The curse was broken through something as ordinary as a new owner, hard work, and a change of thinking." Locking eyes with Albert and sighing with satisfaction at his suppression of superstition, Phil leaned back in his chair as Albert fidgeted with his teacup.

Jericho's Curse

Some contemporary Christians flinch when they discover that curses form part of the biblical worldview. The Israelites no doubt inherited belief in them from their Near Eastern neighbors but with one important difference: While their neighbors' curses were theurgical or magical, persuading a god to do or refrain from doing something, the Israelites' were theological in focus and arose out of ethical considerations. A covenant context replaced a magical background. This is the case of Jericho's water and one of the first miracles of Elisha.

Scripture says the Israelites entered the promised land at Jericho. According to chapter 6 of the book of Joshua, by divine order given to Joshua (Josh 6:2–5), Israel's warriors and seven priests were to march around the city's walls for six days until the walls fell on the seventh day. Once the walls had fallen, the Israelites destroyed the city and its population, with the exception of Rahab the prostitute, her family, and those who belonged to her. They were spared because of Rahab's kindness, hiding two messengers Joshua had sent to spy out the city (vv. 21–25). All silver and gold, along with the vessels of bronze and iron, were considered sacred to the Lord and destined for the treasury of the Lord (v. 19). The Israelites were commanded not to take anything for themselves from the city lest they bring trouble upon their camp (v. 18).

Not everyone obeyed. Some people "broke faith in regard to the devoted things: Achan son of Carmi son of Zabdi son of Zerah, of the tribe of Judah, took some of the devoted things; and the anger of the LORD burned against the Israelites" (Josh 7:1). Achan later would be stoned for his actions (v. 25), and the Israelites collectively would be punished by losing about thirty-six men in their failed first attempt to capture the city of Ai (v. 5). Jericho thus was the place where the people of Israel first sinned against God within a week of living in their new land.

Joshua, the leader of the Israelites, cursed the city of Jericho after destroying it, saying:

> Cursed before the LORD be anyone who tries
> to build this city—this Jericho!
> At the cost of his firstborn he shall lay its foundation,
> and at the cost of his youngest he shall set up its gates!
> (Josh 6:26)

Future residents of this city would pay a heavy price to live there.

A City Rebuilt

That price would be paid by Hiel of Bethel. While Ahab was king of Israel, "Hiel of Bethel built Jericho; he laid its foundation at the cost of Abiram his firstborn, and set up its gates at the cost of his youngest son Segub, according to the word of the LORD, which he spoke by Joshua son of Nun" (1 Kgs 16:34). Joshua's curse would mark this rebuilt city and the people who lived there.

Could the lingering effects of Joshua's curse be found in Jericho's water? While visiting the city many years later, Elisha was approached by its people. They told him, "The location of this city is good, as my lord sees; but the water is bad, and the land is unfruitful" (2 Kgs 2:19). The Hebrew word *ra*, translated as "bad," can also mean "evil," suggesting the water was having dire effects on the people and their land.

Places Hold Curses

Like the fans of the Chicago Cubs and their belief in the curse of the billy goat, perhaps the people of Jericho remembered Joshua's curse and allowed its memory to become a self-fulfilling prophecy in the quality of their water. The initial events of Israel's entrance into the promised land had created a narrative thread that traveled from generation to generation, infecting the city and its inhabitants. We do not know why the water was considered bad or evil, but it makes sense that such a thing would happen in this city because of its history.

Salem, Massachusetts, is a contemporary example of a similar phenomenon. In 1692–93, more than two hundred people were accused of malevolent witchcraft, after an outbreak of mass hysteria. Thirty were found guilty. Historians are confident that all thirty were not witches. All maintained their innocence apart from one, a local slave, whose confession may have been forced out of her. Contrary to popular belief, none of the guilty was stoned or burned at the stake. And the Salem witch trials did not occur in Salem Town—as the town was known at the time—but in Salem Village, an inland hamlet five miles away that was renamed Danvers in 1752.

Historically a taboo subject within Salem, interest in the Salem witch trials was renewed with Arthur Miller's 1953 play *The Crucible*, which retold the story of the witch trials. Then came the television sitcom *Bewitched,* whose seventh season in 1970 was partially filmed in Salem; Samantha, a "real" witch who traveled back to seventeenth-century Salem, used her magical powers to prove the innocence of the thirty condemned witches.

In a visit to Salem, Phil and his wife discovered a thriving witchcraft business that revitalized the city of forty thousand residents, eight hundred to sixteen hundred of whom identify as witches. Phil was made aware again that places do, in fact, hold stories, and these narratives often become self-fulfilling prophecies. In effect, curses are real because people believe in them.

People Hold Curses

And it's not just places that are cursed with narratives. People are as well. Childhood memories and early trauma can shape the personalities of adults, leaving them to believe they are defined, stunted, and disadvantaged by their past. "I'm cursed with the feeling of inadequacy," Carole comments, "because I wasn't gifted with the looks and talents of my older brother and sister. I've lived in their shadows all my life." In moments of honesty, Bill is aware that his seething anger and the chip on his shoulder are rooted in being bullied in grammar school. Dennis laments that his parents' divorce when he was ten years old has left him needy for attention and affection. Nancy's father was abusive to her mother, and Nancy, now thirty-eight years old, is just discovering why she has always dated men who are disrespectful toward women. Adrian suffered severe trauma as a young child and wonders aloud, "Why don't I have any strong feelings about anything?" Each of these five adults proves the falsity of the child's chant, "Sticks and stones may break my bones, but words can never hurt me." Words—and actions—*do*, in fact, cause emotional and psychological harm.

Are we condemned to the harmful words spoken to us? Are we doomed to live out the narratives of our childhoods? Does the past have an unyielding power over our present thoughts, words, and actions? A symbolic understanding of Elisha's salt cure might provide an answer.

Elisha's Salt Cure

The second chapter of the Second Book of Kings narrates Elisha's response to the inhabitants of Jericho when he heard about the quality of their water.

> He said, "Bring me a new bowl, and put salt in it." So they brought it to him. Then he went to the spring of water and threw the salt into it, and said, "Thus says the LORD, I have made this water wholesome; from now on neither death nor miscarriage shall come from it." So the water

has been wholesome to this day, according to the word
that Elisha spoke. (2 Kgs 2:20–22)

Two details of Elisha's curative technique are noteworthy. First, Elisha called for a new bowl. No doubt the old bowls had been contaminated by the water. This could be interpreted symbolically as the need for new techniques and paradigms—as Tom Ricketts used in overhauling the entire Chicago Cubs organization. Breaking from the past requires just that: a *break* from the past. We decide to move on.

Second, the prophet used salt. Salt dissolves in water and cannot be seen—yet its effect is unmistakable. Indeed, the water was made "wholesome," the Hebrew word also being translated as "purified," "healed," or "fresh." Symbolically, this means altering the very taste of the source—reframing the narrative and changing how we think and feel about it.

In one simple gesture, Elisha broke the memory of Jericho's origin and Joshua's curse. The gesture began a new narrative.

The Ministry of Jesus

In his ministry, Jesus offered people the opportunity to break from the past and begin a new narrative for their lives. Matthew the tax collector left his post and became a disciple at the invitation of Jesus (see Matt 9:9). Zacchaeus was called out of the sycamore tree and voluntarily offered to repent of his past fraud (see Luke 19:1–10). The woman caught in adultery was invited to break from her past and write a new narrative for her life with these simple words, "Go your way, and from now on do not sin again" (John 8:11).

And it wasn't just sinners who were invited to break from their past and write a new narrative for themselves. So were "the sick, those who were afflicted with various diseases and pains, demoniacs, epileptics, and paralytics" (Matt 4:24). A leper was cleansed (see Matt 8:1–4). Two blind men were healed (see Matt 9:27–31). A paralytic was told, "I say to you, stand up, take your mat and go to your home" (Mark 2:11). The faith of a woman who suffered from hemorrhages for twelve years was acknowledged, "Daughter, your faith has made you well; go in peace, and be healed of your disease" (Mark 5:34). In Nain, a widow's son was restored to life (see Luke 7:11–17). Lazarus is raised from the dead (see John 11:1–44).

Besides sinners and the sick, those possessed by demons were set free from their past (see Matt 9:32–34; Mark 1:21–28; 7:24–30; 9:14–29; Luke 9:37–43). Mark's narration of the healing of a demoniac in the gentile country of the Gerasenes highlights in a vivid way how dark forces can imprison and isolate a person. The possessed man presented himself naked, living among the dead, unable to be restrained with shackles and chains, and sometimes "howling and bruising himself with stones" (Mark 5:5). Indeed, he appears subhuman, almost like an animal. After Jesus released the legion of demons and sent them into swine, the man was found by the villagers "clothed and in his right mind" (v. 15). He wanted to go with Jesus but Jesus refused him: "Go home to your friends, and tell them how much the Lord has done for you, and what mercy he has shown you" (v. 19). Freedom from demons led to freedom for mission, leading one scholar to call the former demoniac "the first apostle to the gentiles."[3]

The Power of the Past

Elisha's experience with Jericho's water and Jesus' ministry to sinners, the sick, and demoniacs remind us how easy it is to be imprisoned by our past. To break from the past and begin a new narrative sometimes require a healing of our memories. By revisiting a painful event and using a new interpretive lens, thus changing how we think and feel about it, we give ourselves the ability to no longer be defined or disadvantaged by it. Indeed, a demon can be expelled, a curse can be broken, and a healing can be obtained.

Lack of love, the absence of a loving parent during one's formative years, the scars of sexual abuse, living in the shadow of a more

3. N. T. Wright, *Mark for Everyone*, 57.

talented sibling—these are wounds that never really heal. Just like the wounds still visible on the Risen Christ, some have so shaped our present identity that they remain with us forever. Yet, also like the wounds of the Risen Christ, these wounds *do stop bleeding.* They no longer drain us of our emotional and psychological energies. They no longer condemn us to our past. By the grace of God, they become our marks of victory and the very signs of God's healing power in our lives. They become proclamations that "death has been swallowed up in victory" (1 Cor 15:54). "For if we have been united with [Christ] in a death like his, we will certainly be united with him in a resurrection like his" (Rom 6:5).

The wounds of crucifixion stop bleeding and are transformed into the marks of resurrection the moment the desire for revenge is converted into the balm of mercy and forgiveness. That change—or emotional shift—or reframing the narrative—often occurs through the grace of an insight. Sometimes a person arrives at that insight through some form of inner healing: psychotherapy, prayer, membership in twelve-step support groups, dialogue with a loved one or a trusted friend. Albert often suggests to those he counsels that they develop their own personal method of inner healing based upon five important principles.

The Five Principles of Inner Healing

1. The continuing presence of a loving, compassionate Christ

The first principle of inner healing is that it is always done in the presence of Jesus, the Divine Physician. He is the one who heals, comforts, and consoles. The Jesus who wept at the news of Lazarus's death is the same compassionate Jesus who ministers to us. He has an investment in our broken hearts. "The LORD is near to the brokenhearted and saves the crushed in spirit" (Ps 34:18). "[God] heals the brokenhearted, and binds up their wounds" (Ps 147:3). One way of practicing this principle is to begin with the following or similar prayer to Jesus the Healer:

Lord Jesus, you minister to the afflicted, abused, and abandoned. You are the healer of wounded and troubled hearts. I beg you to come into my life and heal me of the psychological harms and torments of my childhood that cause me anxiety. Heal the pain of my memories so I might be set free from the terrors of the night and live in the freedom of a child of God.

O Lord, heal all those wounds that are the cause of the evil and sin in my life. Grant me the grace to forgive the people who inflicted those wounds—my parents, siblings, relatives, and friends. Apply the balm of your grace on the inner sores that continue to ooze with anger, rancor, and bitterness. Help me to live with the awareness that it costs too much to hang on to these hurts and keep fueling a grudge.

In my brokenness and weakness, I have injured others. Heal them before you heal me. May they one day come to forgive me.

Lord Jesus, you know my burdens through and through. I put them in your hands. Grant me the grace never to insult you by taking them back.

Heal, my Lord Jesus, those wounds that cause me physical illness and make me feel unwanted, unclean, and untouchable—like a modern-day leper or the woman with a hemorrhage. I cry out for your compassion and your mercy. Let me touch the hem of your garment.

Above all, Lord Jesus, grant me the peace and joy that come from knowing you are the resurrection and the life. May the healing I pray for make me an authentic witness to your resurrection, your victory over sin and death, your living and healing presence among us. Amen.[4]

2. *A review of the past event*

We must go back to the past event and take another look at it. This is the hardest task of inner healing because we tend to live

---

4. Anonymous, "Prayer for Inner Healing," rewritten and reformatted by Albert Haase, OFM.

"around" our wounds, evading our hurts, skirting our scars. We rarely, if ever, confront them head on.

Mary has a fine reputation at the office. In public, she appears organized, upbeat, and fun loving. But her family and close friends see a quite different side of Mary: troubled, lethargic, drinking too much, constantly drained. Mary has spent most of her life refusing to confront some deep emotional issues that are probably centered on her mother whom she never refers to in conversation. Mary is living her life "around" her wound.

Our external behaviors often betray the fact that we are running away from something or actively repressing something. Sex, alcohol, workaholic busyness, uncontrollable anger—these are usually not the real problems. They are what we are doing *about* the problems. Think of them as aspirins we take to mask the pain of a headache.

The process of inner healing involves avoiding the aspirins and confronting the headache. We come to grips with the present heartache caused by the past.

Many will argue that "returning to the scene of the crime" and "dragging up the past" are fruitless and waste time on things best forgotten. But we must remember that emotional wounds are like physical wounds: They do not heal if they are neglected. They remain and sometimes become infected. Elisha had to return to the spring to heal its waters.

This does not mean, however, that all wounds can—or should– be confronted *now*. We must not violate ourselves and force ourselves to grapple with issues or events that we are not ready to face. To do so can be dangerous.

Healing is not an achievement; it is a gift. When the time is right, the memory will "perk up" to the surface. That is a sign: it is time to begin the healing process. Until then, God has given us our defense mechanisms precisely to protect ourselves from the very issues or wounds that we are not yet ready to confront. Joan's tragedy offers a vivid example.

At an early age, Joan had been sexually abused by her uncle. For twenty-six years, she had repressed the memory of that abuse.

At age thirty, she fell in love with Bill. At times she began to feel uncomfortable during their relationship but didn't quite understand why. She often projected those uncomfortable feelings upon Bill, blaming him for them. These mixed signals strained their relationship. Then dreams began, and Joan would awaken to feelings of stress and anxiety. Finally came conscious flashbacks to the past incident with her uncle. The wound was perking up. It was calling for attention and healing. It was time to face the past abuse.

Healing begins with the journey through the memory to the past—but in the presence of the Risen Christ. We must allow ourselves to enter again into the darkness of the betrayal, the abuse, the hurt, the wound. We expose the entire incident to the light shining through the wounds of the Risen Christ. We recall the details of the experience and the feelings it raised inside of us. At this point, verbalizing the experience to a caring friend or someone in the helping professions can be of utmost value.

3. *The step of compassion*

The third principle of inner healing is the challenge to step through our pain, anger, and hurt to place our feet in the shoes of the betrayer, to understand the heart of the betrayer. Think of the prodigal son parable, where the father encouraged his elder son to break through his resentment: "We had to celebrate and rejoice, because this brother of yours was dead and has come to life; he was lost and has been found" (Luke 15:32). Understanding breeds forgiveness, an important sign of inner healing.

Several questions help in that process of understanding our betrayer. Out of what emotional wound was the betrayer living? What pain filled the heart of the betrayer that would cause a person to react to us or treat us the way the betrayer did? How emotionally healthy is the betrayer? An insight will sometimes plant itself within our minds as we try to understand the betrayer's heart, as we walk in the shoes of the one who betrayed us, as we enter the flames of the betrayer's hell. Only when we understand the weaknesses and imperfections of others can we forgive them with humility and compassion.

Joan met regularly with a counselor. After a number of sessions, she found relief from some of her trauma as she gradually realized her uncle's psychological sickness.

Inner healing begins when we realize that most of the time, most people were doing the best they could. Sadly, the people who shape our broken personalities are broken themselves. Does that brokenness exonerate them from the trauma or injury they inflicted on us? Does that absolve or vindicate adults who deliberately betray our trust? No. The step of compassion has but one single purpose: to walk in the shoes of the betrayer, to realize that crippled people cannot walk without a limp. And life being as it is, we are all limping.

4. *Calling upon the healing ministry of Christ*

After we have called upon the presence of the Risen Christ, lived through the experience again in his presence, and tried to understand the heart of the betrayer, we can then take the next step in the process of inner healing. We turn to Jesus and ask him to minister to us.

The Risen Christ is both the physician and the balm. We allow the healing light that shines through his glorified wounds to penetrate the deep recesses and caverns of our broken hearts. "Christ and the power of his resurrection" (Phil 3:10) will often burn away the ego's need to crusade, to be vindicated, to be justified, to have revenge. And through Christ's healing touch, light appears where darkness once prevailed. Life comes forth as he calls down the wounds of our past, "Come out!"

Sometimes, even after life is restored, there is work to be done. After raising Lazarus, Jesus said to those standing by, "Unbind him, and let him go" (John 11:44). In restoring life to those areas in our past that have so wounded us or become painful, self-fulfilling prophecies, Jesus often enlists the help of others to unbind us. Thus, inner healing is often aided and abetted by professional counseling, spiritual direction, and membership in support groups.

5. *The proclamation of new life*

Over time—inner healing is a process that doesn't occur with the snap of a finger in one sitting—and through God's grace, the wounds of the past stop bleeding. They no longer drain us of our emotional energy. The infections of anger, bitterness, and self-pity gradually fade from our lives. Though we cannot help but look at the world through the wounds and hurts that have shaped us, we begin to realize that it is not nearly as hostile as we originally thought.

Emotions shift. A new narrative emerges. We begin to walk on equal ground with other broken people who are sometimes in need of our forgiveness *again*.

We also find ourselves reaching through our wound(s) to extend a helping hand of compassion to those suffering the same pain or hurt that we once endured—freedom from the past leads to freedom for mission, as the healing of the Gerasene demoniac reminds us. As Joan volunteers once a week at a shelter for battered women, she is very much aware that her past suffering has not been in vain; it has transformed her into an instrument of healing for others. She knows only too well that the God of all consolation has consoled her so that she might console others with the very consolation she herself has received (see 2 Cor 1:3–4).

The final step of inner healing comes when we can announce and witness to our own new life, as Jesus instructed the former Gerasene demoniac. When someone asks Joan, "Where is that bitter, distrusting woman who was sexually violated by the very uncle she so innocently trusted?" she is quick to paraphrase the words of the angels at the tomb on Easter morning, "Why do you look for the living one among the dead? She is not here. She has been raised from the dead" (see Luke 24:5–6).

Elisha's cure of Jericho's waters is a vivid reminder that we are never condemned to the past. Never. No narrative is ever written in stone. Not one. Though the past's tight grip might constrict or burden our hearts and make us feel cursed, our compassionate God continues to offer us freedom from the past through divine grace and the prayer of inner healing.

Reflect

What memories continue to influence me in a negative way? Why do I continue to allow them to define me? Why am I unwilling to face and move beyond them?

Practice

Develop a method of inner healing based upon the five principles presented in this chapter. What feelings and thoughts arise as you bring your painful past to the Risen Christ?

Ponder

> How can we break free of the past? By using it as fuel for growth in the present. If an event from our past remains painful to think about, we should understand that pain as an indication we have unfinished business—not with whoever or whatever else was involved in the event itself, but with ourselves. . . .We don't have to waste time . . . in wishing we could go back in time to change what happened. We only need to find a way to turn that hurt or regret into a catalyst for growth moving forward from today. . . . Instead of painful traumas you'd rather not think about, you should see nothing but opportunity after opportunity after opportunity.
>
> —Alex Lickerman, MD[5]

Pray

O Healing Spirit of the Living God, enlighten me to the memories and past events that confuse, burden, and imprison me. They are often the sources of my resentments, grudges, and anger that lead me to sin. Give me the strength and insight to face them. May your gift of healing set me free. Amen.

5. Lickerman, "How to Break Free," *Psychology Today*.

3

Face Opposition Boldly

2 Kings 2:23–25

"GOD ALMIGHTY HAS SET before me two great objects, the suppression of the Slave Trade and the Reformation of Manners."[1] It's a surprising journal entry written by twenty-eight-year-old William Wilberforce on October 28, 1787. It betrays not only a growing adult maturity but also an emerging desire to put his Christian principles into practice and serve God in public life: It attests to the rediscovery of his interest in evangelical Christianity and his evangelical conversion on Easter 1786 when he came to regret his card playing, gambling, and late-night drinking while at St. John's College, Cambridge. It also was a result of encounters with anti-slave-trade activists, notably Thomas Clarkson, that culminated in a meal on March 13, 1787, when, already a member of Parliament for four years, Wilberforce would agree to the request by seven others to lead the parliamentary campaign against the slave trade.

Responding to this prophetic call would challenge the very foundations of British culture. By the eighteenth century, Great Britain had been deeply mired in the slave trade for more than two hundred years. Eighty percent of her foreign income came from the export of British-made goods to buy slaves, transport the enslaved to the West Indies, and then return with slave-grown products of sugar, tobacco, and cotton. Not only Great Britain's, but also France's, Spain's, Portugal's, and Holland's colonies all relied on this trade.

1. Stetson, *Creating the Better Hour*, 35.

Wilberforce encountered fierce opposition and had to overcome international politics, parliamentary filibustering, and entrenched bigotry. Over sixteen years, he introduced more than fifteen bills to end the slave trade, each roundly defeated. Pro-slavery forces targeted and vilified him. One friend feared Wilberforce would be "carbonated [broiled] by Indian planters, barbecued by African merchants, and eaten by Guinea captains."[2]

John Wesley, the English founder of the Methodist movement, understood the formidable, countercultural task that Wilberforce and his colleagues were facing for the sake of their belief in Christ. A week before he died, Wesley wrote to Wilberforce—February 24, 1791—and compared the monumental challenge of the Englishman to that of an early Egyptian Christian:

> Unless the divine power has raised you up to be as "Athanasius against the world," I see not how you can go through your glorious enterprise in opposing that execrable villainy, which is the scandal of religion, of England, and of human nature. Unless God has raised you up for this very thing, you will be worn out by the opposition of men and devils. But if God be for you, who can be against you? Are all of them stronger than God? O be not weary of well-doing! Go on, in the name of God and in the power of His might, till even American slavery (the vilest that ever saw the sun) shall vanish away before it.[3]

The reference to Athanasius is noteworthy. In the early fourth century, this bishop of Alexandria had to confront opponents who believed and promoted what the Council of Nicaea declared to be a heresy, Arianism. This heresy, promoted by Arius, stated that the Father was one and that the Son and the Spirit were subordinate to the Father. The Son of God was a *creature*, according to Arius, albeit the first and greatest of God's creatures.

Athanasius was bishop of Alexandria for almost forty-five years, and he spent a large part of his episcopacy fighting the Arians. The opposition he faced would lead him to be exiled five times

2. Anonymous, "William Wilberforce," *Christianity Today*.

3. Anonymous, "Wesley to Wilberforce," *Christian History Institute*.

by four different emperors. He spent two exiles in the West, and his final three in the Egyptian desert.

John Wesley knew the vocation to follow God's call in abolishing the slave trade was difficult and complicated much like Athanasius's struggle against the Arians. But he also knew, alluding to Paul's Letter to the Romans as he did, "If God is for us, who is against us?" (Rom 8:31). His words to Wilberforce no doubt were the encouragement and prompting needed for the next sixteen years until the legislation abolishing the British slave trade was finally passed on March 25, 1807. If nothing else, forty-seven-year-old Wilberforce had discovered over twenty years an important lesson of the prophetic call: facing opposition requires fidelity to one's call and a tenacious spirit of perseverance.

Bethel and the Bears

Early on, after he healed the water in Jericho, Elisha learned this same lesson: that the prophetic call involved opposition and required faithful perseverance. While he was on the way to Bethel, "some small boys came out of the city and jeered at him, saying, 'Go away, baldhead! Go away, baldhead!' When he turned around and saw them, he cursed them in the name of the LORD. Then two she-bears came out of the woods and mauled forty-two of the boys" (2 Kgs 2:23–24).

What a strange story! Was Elisha a petty prophet who couldn't handle his baldness being ridiculed? Or were the children mocking his baldness for another reason? Is there a causal connection between the prophet's curse and the she-bears' mauling? Or is the writer attempting to inculcate reverence for the prophet? The reader can only pause and ponder.

The location of the incident gives us a partial behind-the-scenes look at what might have been going on. Located on the north-south mountain road north of Jerusalem, the city of Luz had been conquered by the Joseph tribe (see Judg 1:22–25) and become a part of the tribe of Ephraim (one of Joseph's sons). Even earlier, when Joseph's father, Jacob, had traveled to Aram, he had spent the night there. In a dream, he'd seen a ladder reaching up to heaven with angels traversing up and down. God spoke to him and reiterated the promise to bless Jacob's descendants and give them the land of Israel. In response, Jacob erected a shrine there and renamed the city Bethel, Hebrew for "House of God," for this "is none other than the house of God, and this is the gate of heaven" (Gen 28:17; see also vv. 10–19).

In the period of the judges, Bethel was an important city. It not only was the center of the tribal confederacy, but also housed the ark of the covenant (Judg 20:27).

By the time of Elisha, however, Bethel, the house of God, had become the house of another god. About fifty years before Elisha, King Jeroboam I of Israel, to consolidate his power, had made the city one of the centers of worship for one of the two new gods he had invented. He made two golden calves, placed one in Bethel and the other in Dan, and told the people of Israel, "You have gone up to Jerusalem long enough. Here are your gods, O Israel, who brought you up out of the land of Egypt" (1 Kgs 12:28). He even set up a temple and assigned priests in Bethel so the people could offer sacrifices to the calves (vv. 25–33).

As Elisha approached the city many years later, it is understandable why he was perceived as a threat. Here was a prophet of Yhwh coming to a city where another god was worshiped.

The Gang of Youth

Who were the hecklers in support of this other god? Bible translators have favored one translation of the Hebrew word *na'ar*: "small boys" (New Revised Standard Version), "young lads" (New American Standard Bible), "little boys" (New American Bible Revised Edition), "youths" (New King James Version), "little children" (King James Version), and "insignificant young men" (International Standard Version).

Though English translators have favored "boys" and "children," the Hebrew *na'ar* can also be translated as "young men," "attendants," or "soldiers," suggesting this gang of forty-plus youths could have served as soldiers in a war or counselors to the king. The word describes "behavior rather than age" and suggests a person who "shows youth in his actions."[4] In the words of one writer:

> This was not a crowd of playful children, but a gang of sullen, insolent men and women who had chosen evil and gathered to mock the God of Israel and His word. They were apostates who took delight in ridicule and contempt, hoping to prejudice others against Elisha's message. Their purpose was to run God's prophet out of town.[5]

Because the term can refer to anyone up to the age of thirty,[6] these people were old enough to know what they were doing and therefore posed a serious threat to Elisha and his prophetic call. When they disparaged Elisha's bald head and told him to go away, their voices would have sounded more like an angry mob than a kindergarten classroom.

The gang's jeers were meant to frighten and threaten Elisha. Yet, in fact, the hecklers were the ones threatened, because Elisha was the prophet of Yhwh, the God they did not believe in. His very presence in Bethel could challenge and adversely affect the local economy, which relied heavily upon the worship of the golden calf erected by Jeroboam—much as Wilberforce's challenge to the slave trade affected the British economy.

The criticism of Elisha's bald head probably wasn't just childish name-calling. It could have been an attempt to mock Elisha's prophetic role, because the prophet might have shaved his head as a distinguishing mark of his mission. Or it could have been an attempt to shame the prophet as an outcast, because lepers often shaved their heads.

There is a third possibility for the criticism leveled against the prophet's bald head. Previously Elisha had traveled with and relied upon Elijah, but Elijah recently had been taken by God to heaven. Before Elijah was taken by God, Elisha had been asked by

---

4. "Ask the Rabbi: Naar-ish," *Ohr Somayach*.

5. Roper, *Seasoned with Salt*, 32.

6. Roper, *Seasoned with Salt*, 32.

some prophets in Jericho, "Do you know that today the LORD will take your master away from you?" (2 Kgs 2:5). The grammatical structure of the Hebrew question implies Elijah being taken away from over Elisha's head. The gang's taunts and name-calling could be a reminder that Elijah's absence has made Elisha symbolically bald, because the prophet had no one to guide and protect him. He was now on his own.

Or was he? The Old Testament writer makes it clear that the prophet has divine help by linking Elisha's curse in YHWH's name with the immediate appearance of two hungry she-bears. In the face of opposition, a prayer is apparently heard.

The Cross

Difficulty and opposition are the expectation, not the exception. Jesus preached about this time and again:

- In the Sermon on the Mount, Jesus calls "blessed" those who are reviled and persecuted on his account. Their reward will be great in heaven (Matt 5:11–12).

- His disciples will be dragged before governors and kings and flogged. Families will be torn apart. His followers will be hated by all. "But the one who endures to the end will be saved" (Matt 10:16–22, 34–36).

In the Gospel of John, Jesus openly states this opposition more explicitly:

- "If the world hates you, be aware that it hated me before it hated you. If you belonged to the world, the world would love you as its own. Because you do not belong to the world, but I have chosen you out of the world—therefore the world hates you" (15:18–19).

- "They will put you out of the synagogues. Indeed, an hour is coming when those who kill you will think that by doing so they are offering worship to God" (16:2).

- "I have said this to you, so that in me you may have peace. In the world you face persecution. But take courage; I have conquered the world!" (16:33).

The opposition and hatred of the world are the practical consequences of faithful perseverance to the call of God. The lives of early and contemporary prophets and disciples attest to them.

The Early Church

We see resistance, opposition, and even persecution of the early church. One of the themes of the Acts of the Apostles is the tenacious attempt to squelch and persecute the followers of Christ:

- The Sadducees arrest Peter and John, the Sanhedrin questions them, and they are flogged (Acts 4:3–22; 5:17–42; 5:40).

- Stephen is arrested, questioned, and stoned to death (7:54—8:1).

- The church in Jerusalem is persecuted (8:1).

- Christians are imprisoned by Saul (8:3; 9:2).

- A plot is hatched to kill Paul (9:23–24; 20:19; 23:12–14).

- James is executed and Peter is imprisoned (12:1–5).

- There is a failed attempt to stone Paul and Barnabas (14:5–6).

- Paul and Silas are flogged and imprisoned (16:16–24).

- An uproar occurs in Thessalonica (17:1–9).

Tradition holds that Paul was beheaded in Rome, perhaps as part of the persecution of Christians by the Emperor Nero, and Peter was crucified upside down.

Letters circulating among the early Christians reminded the community of possible resistance and opposition—and sometimes suggested ways to respond. Writing to the Romans, Paul told the Christians to bless their persecutors, never avenging themselves but repaying the evil rendered by their opposers with acts of charity (Rom 12:14, 17–21). He reminded the Corinthian

Christians that their afflictions were signs of "the life of Jesus . . . made visible in [your] mortal flesh" (2 Cor 4:11). He told the Philippians that their struggles and sufferings for their belief in Christ were a "privilege" (Phil 1:29).

The Second Letter to Timothy states, "Indeed, all who want to live a godly life in Christ Jesus will be persecuted" (2 Tim 3:12), while the First Letter of Peter encourages believers not to consider their sufferings a "disgrace" but to "rejoice insofar as you are sharing Christ's sufferings" (1 Pet 4:12–16). The First Letter of John states explicitly, "Do not be astonished, brothers and sisters, that the world hates you" (1 John 3:13). Christians are to find meaning in the resistance and opposition they experience by looking to and identifying with the life of Christ himself.

The Letter to the Hebrews

The eleventh chapter of the Letter to the Hebrews recounts the stories of men and women who remained faithful to God's call in the face of immense doubts and tortuous trials: Abraham's obedience is celebrated not only in his faith journey (Heb 11:8) but also in his belief that Sarah would give birth and in his willingness to sacrifice Isaac (vv. 11, 17–19). Moses is honored because he refused to be called a son of Pharaoh's daughter, "choosing rather to share ill-treatment with the people of God than to enjoy the fleeting pleasures of sin" (v. 25); he "left Egypt, unafraid of the king's anger; for he persevered as though he saw him who is invisible" (v. 27). After noting the success of some famous Old Testament personages, the writer did not hesitate to describe the trials and tribulations of others:

> Others were tortured, refusing to accept release, in order to obtain a better resurrection. Others suffered mocking and flogging, and even chains and imprisonment. They were stoned to death, they were sawn in two, they were killed by the sword; they went about in skins of sheep and goats, destitute, persecuted, tormented— of whom the world was not worthy. They wandered in

deserts and mountains, and in caves and holes in the ground. (vv. 35–38).

The fact of torture and the refusal to accept deliverance "in order to obtain a better resurrection" is an allusion to the incidents that occurred in the time of the Maccabees during the persecution of Antiochus Epiphanes. Those trials did not weaken the faith of the Israelites but strengthened it and led to a clear affirmation of faith in the resurrection of the dead (2 Macc 7:9, 11, 14). The apparent abandonment by God in this earthly life was a radical affirmation of God's positive response in eternal life.

The author of Hebrews then turned his attention to three prophets. The mocking, flogging, chains, and imprisonment is an allusion to the prophet Jeremiah who "was put in the cistern house, in the cells, and remained there many days" (Jer 37:16). He then alluded to Isaiah who, according to Jewish tradition, was martyred by the saw. He alludes to Elijah who went about in a sheepskin (see 1 Kgs 19:19 LXX). He reminded the reader how the Israelites "provided for themselves hiding places in the mountains, caves and strongholds" (Judg 6:2). The author of Hebrews concluded by stating the world was not worthy of such prophetic fidelity (Heb 11:38).

The Book of Revelation

The book of Revelation continues the theme of opposition, suffering, and persecution. Scholars tell us that it was written and possibly edited during a time of widespread and sporadic persecution of Christianity, perhaps between the mid-first and mid-second centuries. The author, named John, was on the island of Patmos and had a vision. He was told to write it down in a book and send it to seven churches.

The text has a threefold purpose: First, John wanted to encourage Christians not to conform to contemporary Greco-Roman society that was beastly, demonic, and subject to divine judgment. Second, he wanted to warn believers of past and future persecutions and trials. Third, he wanted to offer encouragement and hope to the persecuted.

In the letter to the church at Ephesus, for example, Jesus spoke through the author, "I know your works, your toil and your patient endurance. . . . I also know that you are enduring patiently and bearing up for the sake of my name" (Rev 2:2–3).

To the believers in Smyrna, Jesus offered encouragement, "I know of your affliction and your poverty. . . . Do not fear what you are about to suffer. Beware, the devil is about to throw some of you into prison so that you may be tested. . . . Be faithful until death, and I will give you the crown of life" (2:9–10).

Jesus acknowledged the tenacious faith of the community in Pergamum, "I know where you are living, where Satan's throne is. Yet you are holding fast to my name, and you did not deny your faith in me even in the days of Antipas my witness, my faithful one, who was killed among you, where Satan lives" (2:13).

John's vision revealed the torture and martyrdom of believers who "cried out with a loud voice, 'Sovereign Lord, . . . how long will it be before you judge and avenge our blood on the inhabitants of the earth?'" (6:10). The Roman Empire—called "Babylon the great, mother of whores and of earth's abominations" (17:5)—was "drunk with the blood of the saints and the blood of the witnesses to Jesus" (17:6). This last book of the New Testament portrays God's punishment on those who inflicted sufferings on God's faithful. Ultimately, Babylon falls and Christ definitively defeats the devil, leading to "a new heaven and a new earth" (21:1).

Contemporary Opposition and Persecution

That new earth continues to be birthed on different continents in the resistance and challenges faced by those who have been and are faithful to their prophetic calls.

Francis Xavier Nguyen Van Thuan, a cardinal in the Catholic Church, inspired many Christians in his native Vietnam. Arrested for his faith, he endured harsh treatment as he spent thirteen years in prison, nine of them in solitary confinement. During those long years of isolation and imprisonment, Van Thuan discovered he was never alone, because God was present in the darkness. This realization led him to compose messages of hope and courage on scraps of paper. These short messages, 1,001 in total, were smuggled out and instantly gave hope to Vietnamese believers who knew what it was like to suffer for their faith. Released from prison in 1999, Van Thuan died in September 2002.

Fifty-one-year-old Pakistani pastor Zafar Bhatti sold medicines door-to-door and regularly took the opportunity to read the Bible and pray with his customers. He founded and led a small NGO called Jesus World Mission to assist the poor. In July 2012, he was falsely accused of blaspheming the mother of the Prophet Muhammad, arrested, and sentenced to life imprisonment in Rawalpindi's Adyala Central Jail.

Christian Naser Navard Gol-Tapeh was arrested in June 2016 when intelligence police agents raided an engagement party at a house in the Andisheh township of Karaj, near Tehran, Iran. At his trial in May of the following year, the judge charged him with acting against national security through the formation and establishment of an illegal church organization in his home. He was convicted. In January 2018, Naser was admitted to section 8, hall 10 of Evin Prison to begin his ten-year sentence.

Wang Yi, the pastor of the Early Rain Covenant Church, one of the best-known house churches in Chengdu, Sichuan province, China, was arrested and detained by government authorities on trumped-up charges of inciting subversion of state power and illegal business operations. In December 2019, he was convicted, fined, and sentenced to nine years in prison.

In Our Lives

Albert knows from his own experience that opposition to one's call can be more subtle—but just as forceful—than outright resistance, arrest, and imprisonment. He spent eleven years in mainland China. On the surface, he appeared to be just another expat working first as a university professor and later as a human resources director for an international accounting firm. However, his primary reason for being in Beijing was to minister to Roman Catholics. He still remembers that Sunday morning in September 2003 when he left his apartment and noticed a marked security police car parked across the street. That car followed the cab he took for a meeting with some of the people to whom he ministered. For the next two weeks, he would be followed continuously by the same security police car. Asking a local Chinese priest what he thought it meant, Albert was told, "That's the government's way of letting you know they are on to you. It's only a matter of time before they knock on your door and give you twenty-four hours to pack up and leave." Knowing his continued presence was more dangerous for the people to whom he ministered than for himself, Albert abandoned his childhood dream of being a missionary to the Chinese people and returned to the United States for good in January 2004. Fidelity to the call sometimes masquerades as failure.

Of course, you don't need to live in an oppressive country like Vietnam, Pakistan, Iran, or China to experience the cross of oppression that gives birth to a new heaven and a new earth. Many of us experience the cross in smaller, but often just as painful, ways. Refusing to bow to the pressure of overcharging his clients for ethical reasons based upon his faith, William endures snide remarks from his colleagues and missed opportunities for promotion. Aware of Jesus' love for the outcast, Michelle intentionally befriends minorities who feel ostracized and has lost many friendships as a result. Joseph is adamantly pro-life and ensures that others know that his position includes not only supporting the rights of the unborn, but also includes human rights for those detained at the border, housing for the homeless, affordable health care, respect for the environment, and opposition to euthanasia and the death penalty; he is roundly criticized by people who think he's "gone too far." Robin encounters disapproval as she ministers at a woman's detention center—"You're wasting your time. Those women are no-good and deserve to be imprisoned," a friend told her.

Subtle or overt resistance and opposition are the expectation, not the exception. Elisha's experience at Bethel invites us to remain faithful to our call and firm in our conviction that God will ultimately vindicate us. Sometimes in this life, as God did with Elisha and Wilberforce. Sometimes in the next life, as God did with the prophets, Jesus, and the early Christian believers. In either case, our task remains the same: face opposition boldly.

Reflect

Where am I currently facing opposition in my walk with God? How do I respond to this opposition? How is God inviting me to perseverance and deeper trust?

Practice

Google "Contemporary Christians who are persecuted." Choose one of the websites and read about our brothers and sisters who are being persecuted for their faith in Christ. Consider choosing one specific person to pray for every day. Commit to following up on his or her particular circumstances on a periodic basis.

Ponder

> Daniel Berrigan, in one of his famous quips, once wrote: *Before you get serious about Jesus, first consider carefully how good you are going to look on wood!*
>
> In saying this, he was trying to highlight something that's often radically misunderstood from almost every side, namely, how and why authentic religion brings suffering into our lives.
>
> —Ronald Rolheiser, OMI[7]

Pray

Loving Shepherd, there are times when I am mocked, even persecuted, for hearing your voice and following in your footsteps. Other times, I am surrounded by wolves. Grant me the blessed grace to be tenacious and persistent in standing up to my adversaries while remaining firm and resolute in my Christian discipleship. Amen.

7. Rolheiser, "Sensitivity and Suffering."

4

Believe in the Divine Economy

2 Kings 4:1–7, 42–44

"Phil, I just heard an interesting radio interview with Phil Hellmuth," Albert said during a Zoom conversation.

"Who's he?"

"A famous American poker player," Albert replied. "Hellmuth was talking about a poker player he was staking."

"What's staking?"

"Staking is when someone financially backs a poker player to receive some of the profits from his or her winnings. Typically, the backer will pay the cost of the buy-in to a high stakes game, say around $10,000, and the poker player is obliged to return that cost along with 50 percent of the winnings that are left over. In that radio interview, Hellmuth talked about a player he was staking who stole all the winnings. And I'm not talking about a few hundred bucks. It was $28,000 to be exact!"

"That's a lot of money."

"It sure is, Phil. But what stood out to me was Hellmuth's explanation of how ridiculous it was for the guy to steal the winnings. As long as the man was an honest and wise steward with the money, Hellmuth provided for him. When he got into a tight spot and needed more cash, he simply talked to Hellmuth and got what he needed. So the guy didn't need to steal—but in doing so, he violated Hellmuth's trust and ended up losing his financial backing.

"Believe it or not, that got me thinking about how God stakes us. God has entrusted us with everything. And instead of asking us to return everything with an added 50 percent, God only asks that we trust there is enough and share what we have with others."

"That's a challenge because we're often told there isn't enough to go around," Phil commented.

"You're right!" Albert said, "and so when we find ourselves in a tight spot, we hoard what we have like the guy who stole from Phil Hellmuth. We don't trust in the lavish generosity of God who stakes us."

The Widow

God's lavish generosity is celebrated in the story of Elisha and the widow. After his encounter with the jeering gang of Bethel, Elisha met a woman who was desperate.

> Now the wife of a member of the company of prophets cried to Elisha, "Your servant my husband is dead; and you know that your servant feared the LORD, but a creditor has come to take my two children as slaves." (2 Kgs 4:1)

In biblical times, women were considered second-class citizens and were forbidden to own property. The loss of her husband meant the loss of the widow's financial stability. Now she would be forced to rely upon family and friends for support. The potential loss of her children as slaves to pay off her debt highlights her financial straits. According to the economy of the world, she was finished. Her only hope was the prophet Elisha.

Her dire predicament is further exposed when she confesses to Elisha that she has nothing in the house but a jar of oil.

Elisha told her, "Go outside, borrow vessels from all your neighbors, empty vessels and not just a few. Then go in, and shut the door behind you and your children, and start pouring into all these vessels; when each is full, set it aside" (2 Kgs 4:3–4).

The widow did as Elisha commanded and, with the help of her son, began to pour oil into the borrowed vessels from the one full vessel she had. The oil continued to flow until there were no more vessels left to fill.

Elisha then said to the widow, "Go sell the oil and pay your debts, and you and your children can live on the rest" (v. 7).

Using the prophet as an instrument, God miraculously filled several vessels with only one full oil vessel. That multiplication not only paid the debts, thus keeping the children out of slavery, but also supplied the future needs of the family. What seemed an impossible situation of scarcity became a blessing of abundance.

God's Economy

Economics is the social science dealing with the production, distribution, and consumption of earth's limited resources. All economic systems—capitalism, socialism, and communism—are attempts to distribute fairly and justly these limited resources with members of society.

The story of Elisha and the widow reveals another economy at work in the world: a divine economy. And God's economy is a complete undermining of all the assumptions of the traditional economic systems. In this story, God declares that scarcity and limited resources are not the foundational principles of the economic world. When we trust, abundance is! And Elisha is used as an instrument of the bounty of this divine economy.

The Multiplication of the Firstfruits

This is not the only time Elisha was used as an instrument of the divine economy. In a second incident, a servant from the town of Baal-shalishah brought Elisha food from his firstfruits: twenty loaves of barley and fresh ears of grain.

Elisha turned the gift down and said, "Give it to the people and let them eat" (2 Kgs 4:42).

The servant, asking how he could place this small amount of food before a hundred people, protested in embarrassment.

Elisha repeated himself. "Give it to the people and let them eat, for thus says the LORD, 'They shall eat and have some left'"

(v. 43). The story concludes, "He set it before them, they ate, and had some left, according to the word of the LORD" (v. 44).

Again we see the divine economy at work as it upends the traditional economic systems that often leave people in need. When we share our gifts with faith and trust, we discover that God makes up for what is lacking—and sometimes leaves leftovers.

The Miracle of Manna

Both the Old and New Testaments are keen to highlight God as the staker in the divine economy who calls for trust and makes up for what is lacking.

As the chosen people wandered in the wilderness for forty years, God sent manna to them every morning and commanded that the people gather what they needed for that day: an omer's worth—which is clarified as a tenth of an ephah (Exod 16:36)—for each person in their tents. They were not to store up manna for future days because God would provide for them every single day. If they kept the manna overnight, it would become inedible. In return for his lavish generosity as the staker, God only asked for the people's trust.

When each gathered the food they needed, "some gathered more, some less. But when they measured it with an omer, those who gathered much had nothing over, and those who gathered little had no shortage; they gathered as much as each of them needed" (Exod 16:17–18). Every member of the community had provisions for the day. There was no scarcity.

Feeding the Five Thousand

The miracle of the feeding of the five thousand, the only miracle of Jesus found in all four Gospels (Matt 14:13–21; Mark 6:30–44; Luke 9:10–17; John 6:1–15), is the classic New Testament example of the divine economy. God again requires trust and uses ordinary people as the divine economy's instruments. Though

John's Gospel includes some unique details, each narration contains the same basic facts:

- Jesus invited his disciples to a deserted place.

- The crowds followed them on foot.

- In the evening, the disciples suggested Jesus dismiss the crowds so they could buy food in the villages.

- Jesus instructed the disciples to feed the crowds.

- The disciples noted the minimal supply of five loaves and two fish (John specifically notes the loaves were made of barley, perhaps an allusion to God using Elisha to multiply the barley loaves and ears of grain).

- Jesus took the provisions, blessed them, broke the loaves, and handed them to the disciples for distribution.

- All ate and were filled.

- The leftovers filled twelve baskets full (the number twelve is suggestive of the twelve tribes of Israel, and thus the entire chosen people).

- The narration noted the presence of five thousand men.

This miracle celebrates the divine abundance we enjoy when we share what we have with others. No matter how minimal our provisions might be, we can become instruments of God's lavish generosity as God the staker makes up for what is lacking—and then leaves more than enough behind! This is how the divine economy works.

Multiplication of the Rice

Is the divine economy still at work in our contemporary day? According to the *New York Times*, it certainly is. In September 1975, it published a short article about the canonization of the Spanish-born

Dominican friar Juan Macías (1585–1645), with mention of the miracle God wrought through his intercession.[1]

The miracle occurred on January 25, 1949, at the Catholic church in Ribera de Fresno, Spain, the birthplace of Juan Macías. Macías had been known for his devotion to the poor and was affectionately called by the villagers "the Blessed." A volunteer cook was preparing a Sunday meal for children from a nearby orphanage. She had also invited poor families of the parish to pick up a meal at the door. The cook discovered that she had only enough rice and meat (less than a pound and a half of each) to feed the children of the orphanage. Realizing she did not have enough food to feed all the people she expected that day, she asked her deceased countryman Juan Macías, "Will the poor have to go without lunch?" She appealed to the Dominican brother to intercede on her behalf to God. To her astonishment, and that of those working with her, the pot of rice began to overflow. She ladled some of the rice into a second pot. And then a third. For four hours the pot overflowed with rice. In the end, she had enough to feed not only the fifty-nine children from the orphanage but also the one hundred and fifty poor who stopped by for a meal. Twenty-two people witnessed the overflowing rice pot and testified under oath to the multiplication of food. After intense investigation, the Vatican could find no natural explanation for this extraordinary phenomenon. This miracle led to the canonization of Juan Macías in 1975.[2] Daily bread had once again rained down from heaven and was multiplied—but this time in the form of rice.

"Daily" Bread?

Was Jesus asking his disciples to pray for a similar kind of bread in the prayer he taught them?

The Greek word *epiousion*, translated as "daily" in the Lord's Prayer, has long baffled biblical scholars and translators. It is

1. Associated Press, "Spanish-Born Friar Is Canonized by Pope," *New York Times*.

2. Woodward, *Making Saints*, 209–10.

unknown in all Greek literature except for its appearance in the two versions of the Lord's Prayer found in Matthew's and Luke's Gospels; consequently, there are no reference points to ascertain its exact meaning.

In the third century, Origen, a native Greek speaker and a biblical scholar, confessed he did not know this Greek word. He speculated that those who translated Jesus' words from Aramaic to Greek simply did not know how to translate it and so made up the Greek word *epiousion*.

In his translation of the Bible into Latin in the early 400s, Jerome used three different Latin words to translate this single Greek word. When he encountered it in Matthew's version of the Lord's Prayer, he invented a Latin word for it: *supersubstantialem*, "super-substantial." For Luke's version of the prayer, Jerome translated it as *quotidianus*, "daily." In a commentary on the Gospel of Matthew, he used yet another Latin word, *crastinum*, "tomorrow's."

In 1925, a scholar reported that there was a historical record of a fragment of a papyrus, now lost, that had this word on it. That fragment was part of a grocery list of provisions for someone's household. This suggests that *epiousion* could refer to a "daily ration" of some foodstuff.[3]

Given this background and keeping in mind the larger context of Jesus' teachings, the word *epiousion* does suggest "daily" but in the sense of "just for today," the ration of bread needed only for today. Perhaps Jesus was also alluding to the miracle of the manna. Like that daily miracle, "Give us this day our daily bread" is a call to trust in the divine economy.

The translation as "daily" is strengthened when it is placed alongside Jesus' exhortation not to store up treasures on earth (Matt 6:19–20) and his teaching not to worry about life, food, drink, or clothing (vv. 25–33). He calls us to confidently ask his Father for what we need each day. Just for that day. Not for excess. Not for future security. This is a direct challenge to our distrust in the divine economy.

3. Burton, *Abba Isn't Daddy*, 144–47.

Everything Is a Gift

Our distrust in the divine economy sometimes causes us to hesitate to share what we have with others.

Phil remembers once going to a theme park named Cedar Point with his fiancée and soon-to-be brother-in-law. Before the trip, Phil's brother-in-law had offered him a two-liter bottle of Dr Pepper, knowing this has always been Phil's favorite drink. In Phil's opinion, if there is a contemporary equivalent of manna from heaven, it's Dr Pepper. Phil happily accepted the Dr Pepper as the beverage to enjoy with his packed lunch. The group of three set off for the park.

At noon, everyone gathered at the car to eat lunch. As the three ate, Phil noticed a young African American boy who kept eyeballing the bottle of Dr Pepper. Phil quickly gulped his plastic cup of Dr Pepper and poured himself another. Suddenly remembering this bottle had been a gift from his future brother-in-law and sensing the young boy's desire, Phil grabbed a cup, picked up the bottle, and walked over to the young boy. "I do believe you deserve this," he said.

The boy's mother immediately looked up at Phil, smiled, and said, "Sir, you have just made my son's day," and turning to her son continued, "Now, Andrew, tell this nice man 'Thank you.'"

As Phil walked back to the car, he noticed he still had more than enough Dr Pepper to slake his thirst for the rest of the day.

That's the practical expression of the divine economy: a gift was given and received—the gift was shared—and there's still enough to go around.

Everything we have in life is a gift, grace, and blessing that God has entrusted to us. God has staked our lives so we can survive and thrive. As a gift, however, everything we have is also meant to be shared so that everyone has enough to survive. When asked how to prepare the way of the Lord, John the Baptist became the financial advisor for the divine economy, "Whoever has two coats must share with anyone who has none; and whoever has food must do likewise" (Luke 3:11).

If we doubt God's lavish generosity in staking us and believe there isn't enough to go around, we will tenaciously cling to what we have and subvert the divine economy.

The Teaching of Jesus

A parable unique to the Gospel of Matthew gives us another insight into the divine economy and our role in it. Jesus compares the kingdom of heaven to a landowner who went out early in the morning and hired laborers for his vineyard. "After agreeing with the laborers for the usual daily wage, he sent them into his vineyard" (Matt 20:2). He returned to the marketplace at nine o'clock and hired more laborers. He hired again at noon, three o'clock, and five o'clock.

When evening came, the landowner asked his manager to pay the workers, beginning with the last and ending with the first. Each laborer received the usual daily wage. When the laborers who were hired first complained that they had endured both the work and the heat of the entire day and therefore should have received more than the laborers who were hired later, the landowner reminded one laborer of their agreement and said,

> Friend, I am doing you no wrong; did you not agree with me for the usual daily wage? Take what belongs to you and go; I choose to give to this last the same as I give to you. Am I not allowed to do what I choose with what belongs to me? Or are you envious because I am generous? (vv. 13–15)

This parable traditionally has been interpreted as referring to how God (the landowner) treats the grumbling Pharisees who relied upon their "works" (the first hires), and tax collectors, sinners, and followers of Christ (those hired later). The typical moral of the story is—what is important is not *when* you respond to God's invitation, but *that* you respond.

One scholar, however, has recently reminded us that the parables are not necessarily allegories. There is no necessary one-to-one correspondence between the details of a parable and the details of our everyday life. She writes:

> Sometimes a shepherd is just a shepherd, and not a cipher for God; a king may be just a king, a landowner someone in need of workers; and a lost sheep is not immediately seen as a sinner, repentant or defiant.[4]

Summarizing her understanding of parables, she notes how these short stories challenge us to recognize what we already know by reframing our vision. They don't necessarily reveal anything that is new but rather cause us to revisit our values and our deepest longings. Consequently, "they resurrect what is very old, and very wise, and very precious. And often, very unsettling."[5]

This scholar's interpretation of the parable of the laborers in the vineyard highlights the wise, unsettling challenge of the divine economy and the role we play in it. She writes:

> The righteousness of one person or group benefits not only that group, but others as well. Each group needs the other: the workers need money, and the owner needs the labor. . . .
>
> In this parable, the last hired benefit from the contract made with their [earlier hired] coworkers; they benefit from an employer who pays a just wage to those who labor; they benefit from an employer who is generous with his money. Thus, not only do householder and laborer need each other, the work of some laborers benefits the lives of others. In the end, all have enough to eat, and the rich recognize their responsibility to those who are less well off, a responsibility that includes not simply giving a handout, but hiring "workers" who can thus preserve their dignity.
>
> If we look at economics, at the pressing reality that people need jobs and that others have excess funds, we find what should be a compelling challenge to any

4. Levine, *Short Stories by Jesus*, 18.

5. Levine, *Short Stories by Jesus*, 25.

hearer. And in that story, we learn what it means to act as God acts, with generosity to all.[6]

In other parables, Jesus also taught about our role in the divine economy:

- The parable of the rich man and Lazarus (Luke 16:19–31) focuses on the selfishness and callousness of a rich man whose shame is so great, he goes unnamed. We are reminded that we are, in fact, our brothers' and sisters' keepers, and we should care for those who do not have as much as we have. Blindness to the poor at our door leads to eternal torment.

- The parable of the judgment of the nations (Matt 25:31–46) reminds us that the sheep enter eternal life because they shared their food with the hungry, their drink with the thirsty, their clothes with the naked, and their time with prisoners while the goats, who enter eternal punishment, did not.

- The parable of the rich fool (Luke 12:16–21) portrays a rich man's abundant harvest. Rather than share what he has with others, he subverts the divine economy by building larger barns to hoard his grain for his own future security and enjoyment: "And I will say to my soul, Soul, you have ample goods laid up for many years; relax, eat, drink, be merry" (v. 19).

- In the parable of the good Samaritan (Luke 10:30–35), in contrast to the callous insensitivity of a priest and Levite, an unexpected Samaritan, the traditional enemy of the Jews, cares for a victim of robbers and even puts a down payment of two days' wages for his recuperation. And that's just for starters: "When I come back, I will repay you whatever more you spend" (v. 35).

According to Jesus, the divine economy is about a gift given and shared, a give-and-take, a sharing between the haves and the have-nots, the incarnation of God's lavish staking in and through the lives of others. It cannot happen without our cooperation.

---

6. Levine, *Short Stories by Jesus*, 236–37.

God the Great Almsgiver

Saint Francis of Assisi instinctively knew about the divine economy and the role he could play in it. One day, he was returning to Assisi from Siena. Because of his ill health, the saint was wearing a short cloak over his raggedy tunic. He came face-to-face with a beggar. Seeing the poor man's destitution, Francis said to his traveling companion, "I must return this cloak to this poor beggar, because it belongs to him. It was only loaned to me to wear until I found someone in greater need of it."

His companion, however, knew well that the saint himself needed the cloak badly and was reluctant to see him neglect himself while providing for someone else.

Responding to his companion's protest, Francis said, "God the great Almsgiver will consider me a thief if I do not give what I have been loaned to someone who needs it more."[7]

This is how the divine economy works: God is the great Almsgiver who abundantly provides for everyone if we are willing to be the instruments of God's lavish generosity. That's why whenever the saint received anything for his needs from a benefactor, he always asked permission to give the article away if he met someone in greater need than himself. He spared absolutely nothing—cloaks, tunics, books, even the cloths covering the altar.

Francis's awareness of the divine Almsgiver's economy and the role he could play in it fueled his poverty. For the saint from Assisi, the vow of poverty was not a form of self-denial but a radical affirmation that God can be trusted to shower gifts, graces, and blessings in all aspects of life. Toward the end of his life as he sat down to write his Testament, he looked over his forty-four years and noticed God's lavish generosity time and again in people, places, and events. No fewer than six times in this short document, the saint mentioned the divine economy: God "gave me" the gift of penance; God "led me" among the lepers; God "gave me" the gift of prayer; God "gave me, and gives me still" faith in the clergy; God

---

7. This is a paraphrase of a story found in Saint Bonaventure, *Major Life*, VIII:5, 589.

"gave me" brothers and "revealed to me" how to live according to the gospel; God "revealed" the saint's special greeting, "May the Lord give you peace."[8] The poor man of Assisi was well aware of just how rich he was thanks to the divine Almsgiver.

Our Cooperation

And that abundance, freely given by God, is meant to be shared. When we live in the divine economy fully aware of the role we play in it, we discover a world where everyone has enough. And maybe even more than enough. Oil and bread are multiplied. Manna falls from the sky for everyone. Rice overflows. Dr Pepper remains. The poor and disadvantaged receive daily bread.

Remember how the oil stopped flowing when there were no more jars for the widow to fill? It's conceivable that if there had been more jars, those also would have been filled. Remember how only five loaves and two fish were enough to feed five thousand men "besides women and children" (Matt 14:21)? God's lavish generosity is impeded when people selfishly hoard their gifts, graces, and blessings.

Are we allowing God to fill the empty vessels and feed the hungry people we encounter every day? George, an accountant by occupation, does so by volunteering on Saturday afternoons to help inner-city students with their math homework. Sheila sells her paintings at a local art gallery and contributes 50 percent of the earnings to the Salvation Army. Bridget knits "Happy Hats" and gives them away to the homeless people she encounters on the streets of Boston. Joseph is committed to praying for victims of natural disasters in hopes that his prayers of intercession will fuel hope and solace. Evelyn patiently spends Saturday mornings teaching her neighbor with a disability how to bake and cook. With a sparkling personality, Mary Ann smiles, chats with, and calls by name the clerk at the grocery store and never forgets to say, "Have a blessed day." The divine economy is at work in myriad ways.

8. Saint Francis of Assisi, "The Testament," 124–25.

The story of Elisha and the widow reminds us that God not only stakes our lives, but, as the divine Almsgiver, stakes them in abundance. The multiplication of the firstfruits and the bread explicitly witness to the simple fact that we are instruments of the divine economy when we, like Elisha and Jesus' disciples before five thousand, share our gifts, graces, and blessings with those in need. These stories reflect how the divine economy makes abundant the limited resources of our world.

Reflect

In what areas of my life do I subvert the divine economy by hoarding and refusing to share? How can I nurture greater trust that God will provide in those areas?

Practice

Pray over the gifts, graces, and blessings with which God has staked your life. Choose one and intentionally share it with someone in need. As you share it, say to yourself, "A gift was given and received. The gift is shared. Give us this day our daily bread."

Ponder

> God is a god of abundance, not a god of scarcity. Jesus reveals to us God's abundance when he offers so much bread to the people that there are twelve large baskets with leftover scraps (see John 6:5–15), and when he makes his disciples catch so many fish that their boat nearly sinks (Luke 5:1–7). God doesn't give us just enough. God gives us more than enough: more bread and fish than we can eat, more love than we dared to ask for.
>
> God is a generous giver . . .[9]

—Henri Nouwen

Pray

Divine Almsgiver, all that I have are gifts, graces, and blessings bestowed upon me through your lavish generosity. You have staked my life through and through. Open my eyes and ears to the outstretched hand, the infant's cry, and the prisoner's plea that you place in my path. Give me the freedom and trust to share, knowing that when I respond to the least of these standing before me, I am promoting your dream of the divine economy at work in this world. Amen.

9. Nouwen, *Bread*, n.p.

5

Persist in Prayer, Then Trust

2 Kings 4:8–37

Phil will never forget the journey to his first full-time job. At the time, he was an intern at a church, a high school sports official, a part-time homeless shelter worker, and a full-time seminarian. His student debt was increasing, his internship was coming to an end, and he began looking for a full-time job working with the homeless.

An internship opened at a program working with homeless youth. Phil was excited. He immediately applied, even though it required fund-raising his salary, a task that made him feel uncomfortable. He felt confident at the start of the hiring process. However, after weeks of interviews, phone conversations, and long periods of silence, he was becoming disillusioned. "God," he prayed, "I'm not interested in being a millionaire. I'm really not. I just want to pay off my loans and serve the homeless who have no hope."

Phil began wondering why God wouldn't open the door for something he so desired and where he could be so helpful.

"I really wanted to work with these kids even if I had to do my own fund-raising. I kept making it to the next level of the interview process, but it was taking months, and something just didn't seem right. '*You must take care of this, God*,' I prayed. Though I was frustrated, I kept praying and praying for that job."

Phil now admits he wasn't aware of the other possibilities God might have had in store for him. While he was still working through the hiring process at the youth program, the full-time manager position at the homeless shelter where previously he had been working part-time opened. This job was not only in the same field he desired to work but also included a full-time salary with benefits. And then there were the amazing directors and staff, whom he already knew!

Phil applied for this new position, knowing full well his chances for getting it were slim: He only had been with the organization a few months. He had no management experience. He was still a full-time seminarian.

Shortly after applying, the directors interviewed him and offered him the job. He was now able to work in his desired field, learn new skills, have a flexible schedule, and pay off his student loans. "It was a blessing hundreds of times beyond what I could have imagined with the youth job!"

Phil's experience shows us how God is gracious in answering intercessory and petitionary prayers.

"Our Little Soldier"

Cheryl's experience with petitionary prayer was quite different.

"It's been the darkest and most difficult period in my life as a parent," Cheryl said in a flat, monotone voice as her chin trembled. "My heart still is broken."

Albert nodded in the direction of the box of Kleenex as Cheryl struggled to regain her composure. "Take your time," he whispered. "There's no rush."

Silence momentarily descended on the spiritual direction session as Cheryl closed her eyes and wiped the tears from her cheeks.

"James was a gorgeous baby. I remember how Arthur would spend hours admiring all his little features—his fingers, his toes, his nose, his ears—and then would look at me lovingly with a broad smile. 'I can't believe God gave us the ability to create such a thing of beauty. It is simply incredible,' he would say. And I couldn't have been more in agreement.

"For almost ten years, Arthur and I focused all our energies on raising James as best we could. We showered him with love and affection and with gifts on special occasions like Christmas and his birthday," she confessed. With a thin, forced smile breaking through the cracked earth of her despair, she added, "I think we might have spoiled him rotten."

Silence descended again as Cheryl's eyes glistened.

"But then came the symptoms and the diagnosis," Cheryl struggled for air as the wave of grief swept over her. "I immediately suspected something wasn't right. James had fevers, frequent nosebleeds, pain in his joints, swollen glands, and no appetite. I made an appointment with his pediatrician. Six weeks later, he was diagnosed with acute myeloid leukemia, or AML as it's commonly called.

"Arthur and I were challenged to put our faith in the medical profession and in the power of prayer. As a matter of fact, we prayed like we had never before prayed. James's AML deepened our faith and led us to commit to praying together every night for James's healing. I asked friends to pray. I called a local community of cloistered Poor Clare nuns and got James on their prayer list. People in our church said they were praying for him.

"We were lucky enough to get a referral to St. Jude Hospital. We watched 'our little soldier'—that's how we started to refer to James—undergo chemotherapy. Things looked up. Arthur and I thought the situation was improving. The doctors said it was. Our prayers were being answered. We were hopeful.

"And then, two years later, as happens in 20 percent of the cases, the AML returned. Arthur and I increased our prayers. But our little soldier just couldn't fight it off this time," Cheryl sobbed. "Our prayers only got us two more years with James. That was it. Why do parents have to bury their children, Father? It's so unfair. It's the role of a child to bury the parents and not the other way around.

"I remember yelling and screaming at God. '*Why-why-why?*' For months, I was so angry with God. What kind of God does things like this? Why does he allow young, innocent children to suffer adult, grown-up diseases?

"Someone at church hinted that maybe we hadn't prayed hard enough. But I knew we had; we couldn't have prayed any harder. That person said maybe we weren't persistent enough. But we were. We prayed daily. Sometimes twice a day."

Albert did not say a word. He allowed the silence to descend a third time.

"But you know what? I am gradually discovering something," Cheryl continued as she stared off into the distance, her eyes widening. "God wants me to bring all these feelings of anger and hurt and all my questions to him. He wants to hear them all. God wants me to jostle and wrangle with him even though I am feeling crushed in spirit. He doesn't want me to run away or give up, even though I'm tempted to do just that. I just don't understand why I didn't get the healing I prayed for and wanted.

"Believe it or not," Cheryl's tone changed as if the clouds were parting, "I think I've learned above all else that God is faithful. Sounds contradictory and paradoxical to discover that from the death of my son, huh?"

"What do you mean?" Albert asked.

"Sometimes God's fidelity makes our dreams come true: we pray for a healing, and we get it. Other times, in hindsight, we discover God's fidelity in unexpected ways: we don't get the healing we wanted but friendships that we never would have had form and flourish. And those friendships get us through the tough periods of life. And still other times, our prayers go unanswered, and our hopes are dashed, but God still draws close, gradually bringing peace and comfort. It's taking me time to discover that. Arthur, James, and I *had* to keep praying. We *had* to keep storming heaven. We *had* to keep wrestling with God's will. Otherwise, Arthur and I might not have seen the light at the end of the tunnel and the oasis of peaceful acceptance where God is leading us."

Albert listened in reverent silence as Cheryl's tomb of suffering became a womb of wisdom.

A Dead Child

Elisha's experience with petitionary prayer and death reminds us of an important lesson.

The prophet was in the habit of passing through the town of Shunem. A wealthy couple once urged him to have a meal with them. This became a regular ritual "so whenever he passed that way, he would stop there for a meal" (2 Kgs 4:8). Recognizing Elisha as a holy man of God, the wife convinced her husband to build a rooftop chamber with a bed, table, chair, and lamp—the basic needs of a guest room—where the prophet and his servant, Gehazi, could stay when they came for their meal. Because the roof of a house was the place where family and friends would gather under a canopy for meals and relief from the heat that had built up in the house during the day, this was a generous act of self-sacrifice and service.[1]

Grateful for such a gesture, Elisha asked if the Shunammite woman wanted a word spoken on her behalf to the king or the army's commander. Surrounded by her family and clan in her own town, the woman was secure and so declined the offer.

When Elisha asked his servant what could be done for her, Gehazi mentioned that she had no son, and her husband was elderly. So Elisha called the woman and said, "At this season, in due time, you shall embrace a son" (2 Kgs 4:16). Though the woman initially thought she was being deceived, she did in fact conceive and bear a son "as Elisha had declared to her" (v. 17).

One day while working in the fields with his father, the boy, now older, complained that he had a headache. A servant immediately carried him back home to receive care. Sadly, he died on his mother's lap around noon that day. Having nowhere else to turn, the mother placed her son on Elisha's bed, asked her husband for a servant and a donkey, then journeyed to Mount Carmel in search of the prophet.

Finding the man of God, the Shunammite woman fell at his feet. Discovering the woman's tragedy, Elisha immediately told

1. Roper, *Seasoned with Salt*, 56.

Gehazi to take the prophet's own staff, go to the boy, and lay the staff on the boy's face. Highlighting the urgency of the mission, Elisha told his servant, "If you meet anyone, give no greeting, and if anyone greets you, do not answer" (v. 29).

The woman was dissatisfied with this response and protested and persisted. "As the LORD lives, and as you yourself live, I will not leave without you" (v. 30). Elisha consented and sent Gehazi ahead of them on what would be a failed mission with the prophet's staff.

The story continues:

> When Elisha came into the house, he saw the child lying dead on his bed. So he went in and closed the door on the two of them, and prayed to the LORD. Then he got up on the bed and lay upon the child, putting his mouth upon his mouth, his eyes upon his eyes, and his hands upon his hands; and while he lay bent over him, the flesh of the child became warm. He got down, walked once to and fro in the room, then got up again and bent over him; the child sneezed seven times, and the child opened his eyes. Elisha summoned Gehazi and said, "Call the Shunammite woman." So he called her. When she came to him, he said, "Take your son." She came and fell at his feet, bowing to the ground; then she took her son and left. (vv. 32–37)

Elisha's initial attempt to bring the boy back to life was unsuccessful. The body grew warm, but the boy still was unconscious. Taking this as a sign that God did not will to bring the boy back to life, Elisha could have simply given up and left the room.

Instead, like the boy's mother who pleaded for the presence of the prophet and not simply his staff, Elisha persisted. The man of God walked around the room and tried again. Following this second attempt, the boy opened his eyes and was restored to his parents! Elisha persevered and persisted in his relationship with God through prayer and faith, lessons well entrenched in the following stories of his forefathers Abraham and Jacob.

Abraham and the Three Visitors

According to Genesis 18, while Abraham and Sarah camped near the oaks of Mamre, God appeared to them as three men. Following the ancient custom of hospitality, Abraham convinced the men to stay with them for a while so they could rest and be fed. After a feast and the reiteration of the promise that Sarah would soon have a child, the men set out in the direction of Sodom with Abraham sending them on their way.

As they walked along, the LORD reflected on his relationship with Abraham and wondered if he should inform Abraham of the divine plan regarding Sodom and Gomorrah. Deciding he should, the LORD told Abraham that an outcry had arisen because of the cities' grave sin. Consequently, the LORD had decided to visit those two cities to see if the outcry was based on fact (Gen 18:21).

Knowledge of the divine plan makes Abraham a prophet (see Amos 3:7). He is the first person in the Bible to be so named, in Genesis 20:7. One of the major duties of a prophet is the prayer of intercession (see Moses in Exod 32–34, Samuel in 1 Sam 12, Amos in Amos 7:1–9, and Jeremiah in Jer 14:7–9, 13; 15:1).

Knowing the divine plan, Abraham must have worried about the life of his nephew Lot who lived in Sodom (Gen 19:1). He immediately began interceding for Sodom and, by extension, for his nephew. He asked the LORD God:

> Will you indeed sweep away the righteous with the wicked? Suppose there are fifty righteous within the city; will you then sweep away the place and not forgive it for the fifty righteous who are in it? Far be it from you to do such a thing, to slay the righteous with the wicked, so that the righteous fare as the wicked! Far be that from you! Shall not the Judge of all the earth do what is just? (Gen 18:23–25)

The LORD said that he would forgive the city for the sake of the fifty righteous people.

Abraham pressed and persisted in his intercession, lowering the number of righteous necessary to save the city to forty-five, then to forty, to thirty, to twenty, until he reached the number ten. In each case, God responded that he would spare the city from destruction. This incident gives birth to the biblical theme that the innocent effect salvation for the wicked—as found in Jeremiah (5:1), Isaiah (53:1–12), and later applied to Jesus (1 Pet 3:18).

Abraham was willing to risk his own standing before God by his bold, persistent, and tenacious intercession on behalf of the innocent. It paid off—at least partially. Though he was able to save Lot's life despite his nephew's shameful offer of handing his daughters over for the sexual enjoyment of the men who had gathered outside Lot's house, the prophet was unable to save the city of Sodom (Gen 19:1–29). Was the entire population wicked? We can only infer as much. But the text explicitly states that Lot and his two daughters were saved because "God remembered Abraham" (v. 29).

Jacob Wrestles with God

There is a curious incident in the life of Jacob, another of Elisha's forefathers, that has been interpreted, in the tradition of Abraham and Elisha, as an allegory about persistence in prayer followed by trust.

Having sent his wives, maids, children, and possessions across the ford of the Jabbok River, the natural boundary of his twin brother Esau's territory, Jacob was alone. It was night. Suddenly, "a man wrestled with him until daybreak" (Gen 32:24). Seeing that he was unable to overcome Jacob, the man struck Jacob on his hip socket, knocking the hip out of joint. Jacob refused to let the man leave until he received the man's blessing. When asked, Jacob told the man his name. The man responded, "You shall no longer be called Jacob, but Israel, for you have striven with God and with humans, and have prevailed" (v. 28). When asked, the man refused to give Jacob his name and then blessed Jacob. Jacob named the place Peniel, saying, "For I have seen God face to face, and yet my life is preserved" (v. 30). As the sun rose, Jacob limped away.

Reflecting on this incident, the Christian spiritual tradition has looked upon prayer as a symbol for the battle of faith and the triumph of perseverance.[2] Interpreted allegorically, this passage renders some interesting insights about intercessory or petitionary prayer:

- The incident occurs at night. Darkness is a symbol for mystery, for lack of clarity, for the inability to see and know. A person prays and intercedes in the darkness of faith, knowing the answer to the prayer only in the gradual passing of time. Think of Phil's experience of praying for full-time employment.

- The text explicitly uses the verb *wrestle*. Many people subconsciously approach intercessory and petitionary prayer as a struggle, as a vain attempt to strong-arm God or change the will of God. Think of Cheryl and Arthur.

- The wounded hip symbolizes a change that occurred as a result of Jacob's struggle with God. Indeed, there are times during intercessory or petitionary prayer when a person's persistence changes their attitudes, intentions, perspectives, or desired outcomes. Prayer expands the heart and sometimes changes a person's will, not God's.

- It is striking that Jacob tells the man his name. From the biblical point of view, knowing someone's name implies power and dominance over that person since it was believed the name contained the most profound reality of the individual. In a general audience in May 2011, Pope Benedict XVI noted, "When, therefore, in answer to the unknown person's request Jacob discloses his own name, he is placing himself in the hands of his opponent; it is a form of surrender, a total handing over of self to the other."[3] Having interceded or petitioned, a person must trust in whatever outcome God so chooses.

---

2. *Catechism of the Catholic Church*, par. 2573.
3. Benedict XVI, General Audience.

- The trust implied in such surrender and submission is transformative. Hence, Jacob receives a new name, a new identity. Even when intercessory or petitionary prayer is answered in an unexpected or undesired way, the person is changed. Think again of Cheryl and the peace and comfort she was gradually experiencing, even in the midst of her son's death. Think of Phil and the surprise he received.

- The man's refusal to tell Jacob his name is symbolic of the omnipotence of God. No one can dominate the divine.

- In his reflections on this text, Benedict XVI concluded:

> Prayer requires trust, nearness, almost a hand-to-hand contact that is symbolic not of a God who is an enemy, an adversary, but a Lord of blessing who always remains mysterious, who seems beyond reach. Therefore the author of the Sacred text uses the symbol of the struggle, which implies a strength of spirit, perseverance, tenacity in obtaining what is desired. And if the object of one's desire is a relationship with God, his blessing and love, then the struggle cannot fail but ends in that self-giving to God, in recognition of one's own weakness, which is overcome only by giving oneself over into God's merciful hands.[4]

Though the allegorical interpretation of the incident offers some interesting insights, questions remain: Why did the man—whom Jacob later discovered to be God—engage Jacob at night? Was it to put Jacob at a disadvantage? Why did he initially hide his identity? Was it to see if Jacob would wrestle with him? Why did he begin the wrestling match in the first place? Was he testing Jacob's strength of will, persistence, and tenacity? Why did he wound Jacob? Was he acknowledging his divine power over him? Why didn't he simply bless Jacob without the struggle? Was he testing Jacob's deepest desires?

Such questions all point to the darkness—or mystery—of intercessory and petitionary prayer. We can never comprehend why God seemingly delays in answering our requests. We can never

---

4. Benedict XVI, General Audience.

understand why God sometimes refuses our petitions outright. We can never fathom why God sometimes leaves us in the dark. Despite our questions, as Phil, Cheryl, Elisha, Abraham, and Jacob remind us, we are called to be persistent in prayer and then trust by putting ourselves in the merciful hands of God. In that surrender, we are given a new name—we discover again our truest identity as children of a loving God.

The Parable of the Persistent Widow

There is a parable, unique to Luke's Gospel, that highlights both the importance of persistence in prayer and then trusting and surrendering to our loving God. Luke interprets the parable as "[the disciples'] need to pray always and not to lose heart" (Luke 18:1).

In the parable, a judge "who neither feared God nor had respect for people" (v. 2) is hounded by a widow who demands justice against her opponent. The judge initially refuses the widow's request. But finally, speaking to himself, the judge acknowledges the widow's persistence—"this widow keeps bothering me"—and grants her justice "so that she may not wear me out by continually coming" (v. 5). The Greek *hypopiazo*, translated here as "wear me out," is a boxing term that suggests "a punch in the eye."[5] The judge comes across as more protective of his own interests than the widow's.

The parable leaves the reader wondering if God is a petty god who needs to be cajoled and strong-armed. Does God respond to our petitions just to get us off his back? To avoid such interpretations, doing something rarely found in the four Gospels, Luke has Jesus explicitly comment on his own parable:

> And the Lord said, "Listen to what the unjust judge says. And will not God grant justice to his chosen ones who cry to him day and night? Will he delay long in helping them? I tell you, he will quickly grant justice to them. And yet, when the Son of Man comes, will he find faith on earth?" (vv. 6–8)

5. *The Jewish Annotated New Testament*, 137.

The commentary uses the rabbinical technique called *qal wehomer*, a process of deduction where something that applies in a lesser case must also apply in a more important one. If an unjust judge who cares nothing for God or others will grant the plea of a widow who persists in her request, *how much more* will God, who is thoroughly just and loving, grant justice to someone asking for it!

The question that ends Jesus' comment is a reminder of the difficulty of perseverance and faith when God seemingly goes silent, delays, or is unresponsive. The challenge remains: *persist* in prayer, *then trust*.

The Parable of Perseverance in Prayer

A similar point is made earlier in another parable unique to Luke's Gospel. A man approaches his friend at midnight with the request for three loaves of bread for a visitor. His friend refuses, saying the door is locked and his children are in bed. Jesus notes, "I tell you, even though he will not get up and give him anything because he is his friend, at least because of his persistence he will get up and give him whatever he needs" (Luke 11:8).

Scholars note the challenge of rendering the rare Greek word *anaideia* into English. It is translated here as "persistence." It is found nowhere else in the New Testament. Some believe it is better translated as "avoidance of shame" and refers to the friend in bed and not the neighbor in need.[6] In a first-century culture, where a town's honor and reputation were based upon its hospitality, this translation seems better and appropriate.

Jesus' commentary on the parable confirms this:

> So I say to you, Ask, and it will be given you; search, and you will find; knock, and the door will be opened for you. For everyone who asks receives, and everyone who searches finds, and for everyone who knocks, the door will be opened. Is there anyone among you who, if your child asks for a fish, will give a snake instead of a fish? Or

6. Hamm, "Luke," 1068.

> if the child asks for an egg, will give a scorpion? If you
> then, who are evil, know how to give good gifts to your
> children, how much more will the heavenly Father give
> the Holy Spirit to those who ask him! (vv. 9–13)

Again the rabbinical technique of *qal wehomer* is used. Three points are worthy of note:

- The Greek present imperative verbs suggest "*keep on* asking . . . seeking . . . knocking." Because the verbs lack direct objects grammatically, Jesus is not teaching what to pray for but *how* to pray—with tenacity and persistence.

- Jesus is not suggesting that every intercession or petition *will be granted*; rather, he is highlighting the fact that a divine response *will be given*. One should trust in God's loving concern. To avoid shame, God will not deceive the intercessor or petitioner.

- Luke changes Matthew's gift of "good things" (Matt 7:11) to "the Holy Spirit," thus highlighting the superabundant generosity of God.

Both Lukan parables point to a God who is more tender than an unjust judge, more generous than a neighbor who is inconvenienced, and more straightforward than a miserly, cruel parent. Though our experience might say otherwise, because of God's delay or denial of our intercessions and petitions, Jesus challenges us to trust in God's care, concern, and love.

The big questions go unanswered: Why does God respond to some intercessions and petitions immediately, as he did in the case of Abraham and Elisha, and seemingly ignores others, as in Cheryl's case? Why does he delay in responding to others? Why does he respond in unexpected ways, as he did with Phil? The Scriptures encourage us to be persistent in interceding and petitioning God—we wrestle, wrangle, and jostle—and then we trust that God only desires to give us the best. As we struggle to accept God's will at times, Jesus' question is worth pondering: when the Son of Man comes, will he find faith on earth?

Reflect

When did my intercessory or petitionary prayer apparently go unanswered? How did God's silence make me feel? Did I continue to pray for God's favorable response, or did I stop praying? Why?

Practice

Consider some of the crises of the world: climate change, world hunger, human trafficking, sexual abuse of minors, wars, racism, for example. Choose one and commit to praying every day for its abolition. Monitor your feelings about your persistence in prayer and your trust in God's love as the weeks turn to months.

Ponder

> Prayer is not a magic wand! It helps to preserve our faith in God, and to trust in Him even when we do not comprehend His will. In this, Jesus himself—who prayed so much!—is the example. . . . The object of prayer is of secondary importance; what matters above all is [the] relationship with the Father. . . . This is what prayer does: it transforms the desire and models it according to the will of God, whatever that may be, because the one who prays aspires first of all to union with God, who is merciful Love. . . .
>
> We must not cease to pray, even if left unanswered.
>
> —Pope Francis[7]

Pray

Loving God, I can never understand fully the mystery of your being or comprehend your response to my prayers of intercession and petition. Grace me with the Spirit's gift of persistence in prayer, even when I think you are delaying or denying my request, and may I never lose trust in your superabundant generosity. I pray this in Jesus' name. Amen.

7. Pope Francis, General Audience.

6

Be Sensitive to Others

2 Kings 5:1–19

Martin, a devout Roman Catholic, arrived unusually quiet for his monthly spiritual direction session with Albert. Sitting down, he stared at his feet.

Knowing Martin well, Albert asked, "What's going on?"

"Father, I feel so guilty."

"About what?"

"Two weeks ago, I didn't keep the Lord's Day holy. I broke the commandment and missed Mass."

"That's so unlike you. How did that happen?"

"I had every intention of going to Mass. As a matter of fact, I was in my car, and, as I made my way to church, I saw a car parked on the side of the road with its emergency lights flashing. There was an older couple standing beside the car with a flat tire. I continued on my way to church but then something told me to turn around and see if I could help them. So I made a U-turn, went back, and parked my car on the other side of the street across from them. I crossed the street, went over, and asked if I could help. They asked me if I had a cell phone, because they wanted to call one of their grandkids to come and change the tire. I told them, 'No need. I'll happily change it.' It took a bit longer than I thought. By the time I finished and got back in my car, I realize an hour had passed. I would get to church just as Mass was ending. So instead of going to church, I just went back home.

"I feel so terrible about missing Mass and not keeping the Lord's Day holy."

"It seems to me that you *did*, in fact, keep the Lord's Day holy," Albert replied.

"Really?"

"By your own admission," Albert said, "you had every intention of going to Mass. You were in your car and on your way. You saw an older couple needing help and you responded to their need. I think the highest form of obedience to the commandments is love. Love is the 'new commandment' that Jesus talks about in the Gospel of John. That's why Saint Paul says in the Letter to the Romans that all the commandments can be summed up with one word. Love is the fulfillment of the law.

"Let me ask you: what would Jesus have done had he been driving your car?"

Pausing for a moment, Martin replied, "I suspect he wouldn't have had to make a U-turn. He would have pulled up in front of the car, gotten out of his car, and asked the older couple how he could help."

"You're absolutely correct. I've got another question for you," Albert continued. "Would you do it again?"

"I probably would."

"Why?"

"Because it was the right thing to do."

"Then I think you're right with God and shouldn't beat yourself up with guilt," Albert smiled. "You're always so faithful in your spiritual life. Fidelity to the commandments and our spiritual practices should make us more compassionate, empathetic, and loving. Your fidelity came to fruition in a spontaneous way two weeks ago. I bet you that God says, 'Well done, good and faithful servant.'"

Martin looked up at Albert, blushed, and whispered, "Thank you."

Naaman Meets Elisha

Elisha too understood that sometimes obedience to the law called for an apparent disobedience for the sake of compassion and empathy.

The fifth chapter of the Second Book of Kings records Elisha's encounter with a military commander from Aram named Naaman. Naaman was well respected as a mighty warrior and leader in his country. Unfortunately, he had leprosy.

One day, one of the young girls he had captured during a raid in Israel mentioned to Naaman's wife that the warrior could be healed if he visited the prophet in Samaria. Desiring a cure, Naaman received permission from the king of Aram to visit the king of Israel. He was given a letter of introduction that read, "When this letter reaches you, know that I have sent to you my servant Naaman, that you may cure him of his leprosy" (2 Kgs 5:6).

Upon reading the letter, the king of Israel tore his clothes in frustration. "Am I God, to give death or life, that this man sends word to me to cure a man of his leprosy?" (v. 7), he rhetorically asked. He suspected the king of Aram was trying to start a quarrel.

When Elisha heard of the king's response, Elisha sent him a simple message: "Let him come to me, that he may learn that there is a prophet in Israel" (v. 8).

Arriving at the prophet's house with his retinue, Naaman was told by Elisha's messenger to go wash seven times in the Jordan River. The commander felt disrespected. He was angry that Elisha did not come out of his house and directly intercede on his behalf. He asked, "Are not Abana and Pharpar, the rivers of Damascus, better than all the waters of Israel? Could I not wash in them, and be clean?" (v. 12).

Naaman's servants, however, urged him to follow Elisha's advice. The warrior submitted, followed Elisha's instructions, and "his flesh was restored like the flesh of a young boy, and he was clean" (v. 14).

With the miracle accomplished, we expect the author of the Second Book of Kings to move on to the next story in the Elisha cycle as has been his custom. But he doesn't. Unlike the other stories where we are not told how the people react after the water is healed, the oil is multiplied, or the child is brought back to life, we are provided with an added curious exchange between the cured Naaman and the prophet Elisha.

A Twinge of Conscience

After Naaman was healed, he approached Elisha and proclaimed his new faith: "Now I know that there is no God in all the earth except in Israel; please accept a present from your servant" (2 Kgs 5:15). What a turn of events! Naaman was from Aram where the god Hadad was worshiped under the title Rimmon, the god of storm and war. His healing in the Jordan River not only changed his life but also his faith. In his enthusiasm, he offered a gift to the prophet who twice refused it.

Having his gift refused, Naaman had two requests. First, acknowledging Yhwh as Lord of all the earth but realizing he is the God of Israel in a special way, he asked Elisha to let him take home two mule-loads of Israelite soil upon which to build the altar where he would worship Yhwh in his home city of Damascus. This request arose out of the ancient belief that each god exercised only local influence over specific lands (see 1 Sam 26:19; 1 Kgs 20:23; 2 Kgs 17:26).

His second request arose out of a twinge of conscience.

> But may the LORD pardon your servant on one count: when my master goes into the house of Rimmon to worship there, leaning on my arm, and I bow down in the house of Rimmon, when I do bow down in the house of Rimmon, may the LORD pardon your servant on this one count. (2 Kgs 5:18)

Due to Naaman's position in the royal court, custom and courtesy demanded that he accompany his king to the house of Rimmon. But now believing in the one true God of Israel, Naaman had placed himself in a moral dilemma. How could he continue to assist the king in bestowing honor on a deity that the warrior himself now knew to be false? He was asking for understanding and compassion and leniency—and forgiveness.

Knowing that the prophets took idolatry very seriously, the contemporary reader can almost anticipate Elisha's response. Will the prophet expect Naaman to disengage from his royal court duties and thus avoid the sin of idolatry? Might he advise the commander to abandon his family and country and remain in Israel where he would not be tempted to feign obeisance? Elisha's response is surprising and catches the contemporary reader off guard. Showing what can only be described as an extraordinary sensitivity for Naaman's situation and perhaps acknowledging the depth of the commander's faith, Elisha simply offered Naaman three words, "Go in peace" (2 Kgs 5:19), thus approving his participation in the ritual. Obedience to the First Commandment gave way to empathetic understanding.

Sticklers and Slackers

This empathetic understanding of the other's situation and the freedom from legalism it represents were embedded in the ministry of Jesus. They often were sources of friction between Jesus and the Pharisees. Here's one telling incident that captures this conflict.

> And as [Jesus] sat at dinner in the house, many tax collectors and sinners came and were sitting with him and his disciples. When the Pharisees saw this, they said to his disciples, "Why does your teacher eat with tax collectors and sinners?" But when he heard this, he said, "Those who are well have no need of a physician, but those who are sick. Go and learn what this means, 'I desire mercy, not sacrifice.' For I have come to call not the righteous but sinners." (Matt 9:10–13)

In the culture of the first century, a meal was a ritual for a Jew to demonstrate faith and devotion to God. The washing of hands, the cleansing of eating utensils, and the preparation of the food were all determined by religious law. One's fidelity was expressed in the kitchen.

And at the table, the meal displayed kinship and friendship. To maintain ritual purity, a Jew would eat only with guests who themselves were ritually pure according to the law, a condition that tax collectors and sinners, by definition, were not. By eating with such people, Jesus knowingly and deliberately violated the religious law, rendering himself ritually impure. Hence, the raised eyebrows and question of the Pharisees.

Jesus, however, understood that there are more important issues at stake. There are times when obedience to the law must give way to compassion, empathy, and love. Therefore he responded to the Pharisees by explaining that he came for those who are sick, not those who appear to be righteous in the sight of God.

Such actions raised the hackles of the Pharisees. Time and again, they accused Jesus of being a religious slacker:

- To test Jesus, the Pharisees brought a woman caught in adultery to Jesus and asked his opinion about the Mosaic law that required her to be stoned. Jesus challenged their innocence and refused to support the Mosaic sentence (John 8:3–11).

- A woman who was a public sinner heard that Jesus was dining at the home of Simon the Pharisee. She arrived unannounced and began to anoint the feet of Jesus. The Pharisee immediately criticized Jesus for allowing the woman to touch him, rendering him unclean. Echoing Elisha, Jesus tells the woman to "go in peace" (Luke 7:36–50).

- When they saw Jesus' hungry disciples violate the Sabbath by plucking heads of grain, the Pharisees pointed out the disciples' guilt. Jesus responded with sensitivity by reminding the Pharisees of the actions not only of David and his companions but also the contemporary priests of the temple (Matt 12:1–8).

- The Pharisees accused Jesus of breaking the Sabbath by healing a man with a withered hand. Using the example of a sheep who had fallen into a pit on the Sabbath, Jesus taught that the Sabbath law had to give way to good actions (Matt 12:9–14).

- While dining on the Sabbath at the home of a leader of the Pharisees, Jesus healed a man with dropsy. Sensing the guests' disapproval, Jesus reminded them they would do the same if their child or ox had fallen into a well on the Sabbath. The guests responded with silence (Luke 14:1–6).

Jesus, on the other hand, did not hesitate to accuse the Pharisees of being religious sticklers whose legalistic mentality threatened authentic devotion to God:

- When the Pharisees and some scribes criticized his disciples for not washing their hands before eating, Jesus challenged their obsessive emphasis on the tradition of the elders over the commandments of God (Mark 7:1–23).

- Jesus noted how the Pharisees missed the real purpose of religious practice when he said, "Woe to you, scribes and Pharisees, hypocrites! For you tithe mint, dill, and cummin, and have neglected the weightier matters of the law: justice and mercy and faith. It is these you ought to have practiced without neglecting the others" (Matt 23:23).

- He succinctly challenged them with these words, "Now you Pharisees clean the outside of the cup and of the dish, but inside you are full of greed and wickedness. You fools! Did not the one who made the outside make the inside also?" (Luke 11:39–40).

Jesus made it clear that there are virtues more important than mere obedience: justice, mercy, compassion, empathy, love, and faith. Such freedom from legalism, as we saw in Elisha's response to Naaman, requires a deep understanding of religious laws and a keen empathetic sensitivity to others.

Saint Paul and the Corinthians

Saint Paul gives us a practical example of both that deep understanding of religious laws and that keen empathetic sensitivity to others with his handling of an issue raised by the Corinthians.

Corinth was a bustling metropolis with many pagan temples and numerous images of heavenly powers and emperors who were considered divine. These so-called gods were everywhere, and recent converts to the Christian faith—whom Paul calls "weak believers" (1 Cor 8:11)—still might have felt the psychological pull of superstitions and pagan concepts even though they had come to believe in the one God and the Lord, Jesus Christ.

Much of the social life in such pagan cities as Corinth centered on cultic banquets in temples where meat would have been sacrificed to the temple's god and then consumed. Or private dinner parties where the leftover sacrificed meat would have been sold to local butcher shops that would then resell it to others.

The Corinthian Christian community had internal factions; with those factions came disagreements. One of the contested issues was food offered to idols, especially meat.

Why meat? Perhaps it was because there were many poor members in the Corinthian community (see 1 Cor 1:26–27; 11:17–22). One of the few opportunities for the poor to procure meat would have been their obtaining the leftovers from civic celebrations or athletic games. Or perhaps they could be present at a meeting hosted in a local pagan temple. The conundrum in these cases was that this meat would have been offered to idols.

The community had three questions for Paul: Could believers eat meat bought in the marketplace that was probably originally offered in sacrifice at a pagan temple? Could community members accept dinner invitations in the rented banquet rooms of pagan temples where there would be a sacrificial libation to the god in whose temple they were? (A situation quite analogous to Naaman's dilemma.) Could believers accept dinner invitations to the homes of unbelievers, perhaps even of nonbelieving in-laws (see 1 Cor 7:12–16)?

Paul offers a carefully crafted response to these questions in the First Letter to the Corinthians. He begins by quoting a popular slogan of his day, "All of us possess knowledge" (8:1). He notes the potential damaging effect of knowledge: it can lead to arrogance that can consequently destroy the spirit of the community instead of building up the community with love (v. 2).

Paul acknowledges what the Corinthians already know: "no idol in the world really exists" and "there is no God but one" (v. 4). Though there may be many "so-called gods in heaven and on earth," (v. 5), there is only "one God, the Father" and "one Lord, Jesus Christ" (v. 6). This was the knowledge Paul had communicated to the community.

But this knowledge was not fully ingrained in every believer. Paul refers to the newly converted, the "weak believers" whose "conscience is weak" (vv. 10–11). These believers knew the food available for them to eat was food that had been offered to an idol. To eat such food, they believed, had a religious significance. It raised a moral dilemma that violated their conscience—to use Paul's expression, "their conscience, being weak, is defiled" (v. 7).

This apostle to the gentiles notes the indifference to eating and the knowledge he has gained: "Food will not bring us close to God. We are no worse off if we do not eat, and no better off if we do" (v. 8).

However, highlighting not only his keen understanding of the law but also his empathetic sensitivity to the newly converted, Paul offers this caveat:

> But take care that this liberty of yours does not somehow become a stumbling block to the weak. For if others see you, who possess knowledge, eating in the temple of an idol, might they not, since their conscience is weak, be encouraged to the point of eating food sacrificed to idols? So by your knowledge those weak believers for whom Christ died are destroyed. But when you thus sin against members of your family, and wound their conscience when it is weak, you sin against Christ. Therefore, if food is a cause of their falling, I will never eat meat, so that I may not cause one of them to fall. (vv. 9–13)

Paul believed that our freedom doesn't give carte blanche to always do as we please. Our freedom must be rooted in a sensitivity to others. It must never cause scandal or division. Even though our knowledge is based upon fact, if it leads to doing something that is an obstacle for someone with a weaker conscience, we sin "against Christ"—that phrase referring to the whole community of believers who are later identified as the body of Christ (see 1 Cor 12:12). Exercising one's freedom, no matter how legitimate, must always be subordinate to the obligations of mutual charity.

This charitable sensitivity toward the other was evident when Elisha sent Naaman on his way, even though he knew the warrior would accompany his king to the temple of Rimmon. Not accompanying his king might have at least compromised his position or at most caused scandal in the royal court. The prophet was confident that Naaman now believed in Yhwh and knew Rimmon as a "so-called" god, to use Paul's expression. The bottom line is the unity of Naaman's community.

Paul, the apostle to the gentiles, quickly adds in the same letter to the Corinthians:

> For though I am free with respect to all, I have made myself a slave to all, so that I might win more of them. To the Jews I became as a Jew, in order to win Jews. To those under the law I became as one under the law (though I myself am not under the law) so that I might win those under the law. To those outside the law I became as one outside the law (though I am not free from God's law but am under Christ's law) so that I might win those outside the law. To the weak I became weak, so that I might win the weak. I have become all things to all people, that I might by all means save some. I do it all for the sake of the gospel, so that I may share in its blessings. (1 Cor 9:19–23)

The mature believer is required to be considerate and empathetic to each and every individual in the community—"to become all things to all people." True freedom finds expression in the ability to adapt to the needs of others and never cause scandal or division. Think of Martin's spontaneous act of helping the older couple with a flat tire. Think of Jesus' challenge that the Sabbath must never hinder acts of love and compassion.

Though the Jews were bound to the prescriptions of the Torah, Paul was willing to bind himself to them even though his faith in Christ exempted him from the laws of the five books of the Pentateuch. His actions arose from a desire to "win" those under the law, outside the law, and the weak—for the sake of their salvation and the building up of the community. Again, the unity of the community takes precedence—eloquently expressed, as Paul reminds the Romans, as Jesus' new commandment. Love is the fulfillment of the law (see Rom 13:10).

Saint Francis and a Hungry Friar

Bonaventure, the official biographer of Saint Francis, narrated an incident in the life of the saint from Assisi that offers yet another practical example of the empathetic sensitivity we are challenged to have toward others. It captures Paul's understanding of becoming all things to all people.

In the Middle Ages, fasting, asceticism, and self-mortification were considered important spiritual practices. We know Saint Francis was exceptionally strict with the discipline of his body. In his biography, Bonaventure states, "He used to call his body Brother Ass, for he felt it should be subjected to heavy labor, beaten frequently with whips, and fed with the poorest food."[1] Over time, the saint would regret how stern he had been on his body and apologize to it for his mistreatment.

The incident narrated by Bonaventure probably occurred later in Francis's life since the biographer introduces it by stating, "Although he energetically urged the brothers to lead an austere life, he was not pleased by an intransigent severity that did not put on a heart of piety and was not seasoned with the salt of discernment."[2]

---

1. Bonaventure, *Major Life V: 6*, 564.
2. Bonaventure, *Major Life V: 7*, 564.

One night during a time of fasting, one of the brothers was so hungry he was unable to fall asleep. Saint Francis understood what was happening and called the brother to the table. He put a loaf of bread in front of the brother. So that the brother would not be ashamed or embarrassed, the saint broke his fast and began to eat. He then invited the brother to do the same. Bonaventure concludes, "The brother put aside his embarrassment, took the food, overjoyed that, through the discerning condescension of his shepherd, he had both avoided harm to his body, and received an edifying example of no small proportion."[3]

The simple incident shows Francis's extraordinary sensitivity to the hungry brother. Francis was emotionally free to break his own fast for the sake of the other. He satisfied his hunger for the sake of the hungry. This preserved the brother's dignity and saved him from shame and embarrassment. Over the years, the saint had come to realize that the most effective spiritual practices were charity, compassion, and empathy. In practicing these virtues, he gives us an edifying example of "becoming all things to all people."

Like Martin, Elisha, Jesus, Paul, and Saint Francis, we sometimes find ourselves grappling with a moral dilemma: do I constrict my heart with a strict interpretation of the religious law as I know it, or do I expand it with sensitivity and empathy toward the other? Our spiritual tradition makes it clear that the highest form of obedience is love. In the famous words of the Carmelite mystic John of the Cross, "When evening comes, you will be examined in love."[4]

3. Bonaventure, *Major Life V: 7*, 565.
4. St. John of the Cross, *The Sayings of Light*, #60, 90.

Reflect

Under what circumstances do I tend to be a stickler? A slacker? When do I experience the tension between obedience to the Ten Commandments and Jesus' command to love? How do I resolve that tension?

Practice

For four consecutive Sundays, as you travel to church, be attentive to anyone in possible need. Do the same once you arrive at the church's parking lot and walk to the church's entrance. If you see someone in need, respond in an appropriate way, even if it means being late or missing the service. Afterward, reflect on the experience and notice any feelings or thoughts that arise.

Ponder

> Pharisaism can only work if your religion keeps you "unconscious" and on cultural cruise control. Such immature religion is almost always preoccupied with externals, formulas, exact rituals performed exactly, costumes, roles, and titles—and obedience and group loyalty as the highest virtues instead of love. . . .
>
> *When you have not had any internal experience of God and grace, you almost always overcompensate with external window dressing.* The "window dressings" are not wrong in themselves, but do tend to make *nonessentials into the essentials that we obsess about and divide over.*
>
> Most of us begin with lessons and laws, and then we stay there forever; we never make it to the Spirit.
>
> —Richard Rohr, OFM[5]

5. Richard Rohr, OFM, *Eager to Love*, 112–13.

Pray

Spirit of the Living God, freedom resides in your presence. Unshackle me from a legalism that constricts my heart and leads to atrophy. Stretch my heart's size so I can spontaneously and unhesitatingly respond to the needs of others with care, sensitivity, and empathy, knowing full well that the highest form of obedience is love. In Jesus' name, I pray. Amen.

7

Bring the Small Stuff to God

2 Kings 6:1–7

"I AM SO IRRITATED with myself." That's how Patrick started one of his spiritual direction sessions with Albert.

"Why?"

"In my family's move to our new home, I misplaced my favorite jacket. It was a gift from my deceased father and has lots of sentimental value. I've looked high and low for it. It's gone. I've lost it."

"I'll say a prayer that you find it."

"Thanks," Patrick replied.

"Why don't you ask God to help you find it?" Albert asked.

"Listen, Father Albert, with wildfires, famines, and flooding, I think God has more important things to be concerned about than my favorite jacket!"

"Well, then, here's another idea: ask for the help of the Franciscan Saint Anthony of Padua."

"*W-h-a-t?*"

"In my Catholic tradition," Albert explained, "we have special intercessors for special needs. We call them patron saints. For instance, if you are praying for someone who has cancer, you might want to ask the fourteenth-century Saint Peregrine Laziosi to intercede with God for a healing on the person's behalf because Saint Peregrine himself was cured of cancer. When I'm writing a book, I always pray to Saint Francis de Sales, patron saint of writers and journalists, to intercede on my behalf with the Holy Spirit so I can be inspired. We jokingly call Saint Joseph, the foster father of Jesus, the best real estate agent in the world, because he's the saint you pray to when you want to sell your house.

"Believe it or not—I know this sounds weird," Albert continued with a sheepish grin, "when you lose something, Saint Anthony of Padua is your man, because he's the patron saint of lost objects. I like to tell people he's the manager of the Lost and Found Department in heaven. And the simple prayer I always pray is, 'Tony, Tony, come around. Something's lost that must be found!' I'm telling you, Patrick, it works almost all the time." Albert leaned back in his chair and chuckled.

"I don't know, Father. That *does* sound weird. But maybe I'll follow your suggestion and ask God directly."

"That's a great idea. But also think about asking Saint Anthony for help. It sure wouldn't hurt. Praying to a patron saint for their help and intercession before God is like having a person of influence working for you behind the scenes. Just as people ask us to pray and intercede with God for their intentions, so too we can ask members of the communion of saints—that 'great cloud of witnesses' as the Letter to the Hebrews calls them—to intercede on our behalf with God.

"And the fact that there's a patron saint for just about everything, from farmers (Saint Isidore) to fishermen (Saint Andrew the Apostle), firefighters (Saint Florian) to florists (Saint Thérèse of Lisieux), and flight attendants (Saint Bona of Pisa) to funeral directors (Joseph of Arimathea)," Albert continued, "is a vivid reminder that God's care and concern are embedded in the minutia of our lives. God yearns to hear about the small stuff."

A week later, Albert received a text from Patrick.

Mission accomplished. Jacket found!

Albert was left wondering if the success was due to his own prayers or Patrick's—or Saint Anthony's.

The Lost Axe Head

There's a short, seemingly insignificant story about Elisha that celebrates God's investment in the small stuff of our lives.

The prophets for whom Elisha was responsible approached the man of God and noted the obvious: "As you see, the place where we live under your charge is too small for us" (2 Kgs 6:1). They suggested they go to the Jordan, collect some logs, and build there a larger place to live. Elisha gave his approval and when asked, agreed to accompany them.

As one of the prophets was cutting down a tree, "his axe head fell into the water; he cried out, 'Alas, master! It was borrowed'" (2 Kgs 6:5). The prophet's distress was threefold: The axe did not belong to him and therefore had to be returned. It was made of iron (v. 6), a rare and expensive metal at the time. He could never have afforded to purchase a replacement axe with the meager earnings of a prophet.

This must have felt like an insurmountable problem. We can only imagine the questions that streaked across this prophet's mind: *Should I run? Will I be forced to work as a slave until I can afford to pay for a replacement axe? Is my time as a prophet finished?* And then perhaps the bigger questions: *Does God care about what has happened to me? Should I pray for a miracle?*

This is not a natural disaster, a war, or an injustice. It's not a poor widow with a debt to pay, a dead child, or someone with leprosy, as found in other stories from the Elisha cycle. This is a story about one man who has lost an iron axe head. Would God be concerned about such a trifling matter?

The Response and Recovery

Indeed, God was. Acting as an intercessor, Elisha calmly asked the prophet, "Where did it fall?" (2 Kgs 6:6). After the man led Elisha to the place where the axe head sunk, Elisha "cut off a stick, and thew it in there, and made the iron float. He said, 'Pick it up.' So he reached out his hand and took it" (v. 7).

Elisha didn't hesitate to act. He performed a miracle and brought the sunken axe head back to the surface where the man could retrieve it.

Even careful readers could easily overlook this story or miss its meaning. Consisting of only seven verses, the story is sandwiched between two dramatic and longer stories—the healing of leprous Naaman and the failed attack of the Aramean army. Perhaps the author deliberately intended for readers to tip their heads to the side and wonder why such a small event was remembered and recorded in the grand scheme of Elisha's life.

The Golden Legend

Between 1259 and 1266, the archbishop of Geneva, Jacobus de Voragine, compiled the popular biographies and traditional lore about saints venerated in his time. This compilation, added to over the centuries, has come to be known in the history of Christian spirituality as *The Golden Legend*. With the invention of printing in the 1450s, editions appeared not only in Latin but also in every major European language. The first English translation appeared in 1483.

The forty-ninth chapter of *The Golden Legend* tells the story of Saint Benedict of Nursia, the founder of Western monasticism. Here's the ninth story recorded in that chapter:

> It once happened that a man was cutting bushes and thorns around the monastery. Suddenly, his axe or instrument of iron that he was using, sprang out of its handle and fell into deep water. Then the man cried out, distressed about his tool. St. Benedict saw the man's anguish. So the saint took the handle and threw it into the water. Soon the iron came up and began to swim until it entered back into the handle.[1]

The reader cannot help but notice the strong resemblance to the Elisha story: The iron tip of an axe falls into water. The user of the axe cries out. A man of God is aware of the person's distress. The iron tip is miraculously restored to the handle. This legend about Saint Benedict clearly follows the pattern of the Elisha story.

1. Translation from the Latin by Albert Haase, OFM.

So what's the point of the Elisha story? Why would it influence a thirteenth-century legend about a sixth-century monk?

How Big Is Your God?

Perhaps the answer can be found in the mystery of God's relationship with us.

Written in 1952, J. B. Phillips's *Your God Is Too Small* continues to strike a chord with thousands of contemporary readers. The author explores numerous images of God and notes their inadequacy. These images include:

- Resident Policeman: God is reduced to that nagging, inner voice of conscience that has been influenced by one's upbringing, training, and propaganda.

- Parental Hangover: one's image of God is based upon the experience with one's parents.

- Grand Old Man: this is a God of reverence and respect but disinterested in the complexities and problems of daily life.

- Meek and Mild: this image of God is woolly and sentimental.

- Absolute Perfection: God is 100 percent perfectionistic and requires the same from believers.

- Heavenly Bosom: this God encourages escape from life and its challenges.

- God-in-a-Box: this God is tamed and contained in a man-made box with neat labels.

- Managing Director: this is a lofty, splendid God who is too busy to be interested in a single human life.

- Secondhand God: this is the God found in books, films, and Broadway plays.

- Perennial Grievance: this is a God who rewards good and punishes evil as in a well-run kindergarten.

- Pale Galilean: this God of prohibitions is cramped, narrow, and joyless.

- Projected Image: this God is a magnification of our own good qualities.

- God-in-a-Hurry: unlike the biblical God, who was never in a hurry, never impressed by numbers, never a slave of the clock, a God of long preparation and careful planning, this God works with lightning speed.

- God for the Elite: this God is only interested in the mystic and the spiritual "privileged class."

- God without Personality: this is a depersonalized God who becomes the Ultimate Bundle of Highest Values.

None of these images adequately expresses the mystery of God and God's relationship with us. Though some might contain a sliver of truth, each one ultimately makes God puny and picayune.

What does a puny, picayune God look like? A puny, picayune God creates and then washes his hands of creation. A puny, picayune God needs to be appeased. A puny, picayune God retaliates with a tit for tat. A puny, picayune God holds on to anger and is hesitant to forgive. A puny, picayune God is boxed in by theology, doctrines, dogmas, and religious beliefs.

Edward's God

One of Albert's spiritual directees shows how a puny, picayune God is alive and well.

Edward once asked Albert about his prayer life.

"It consists of two tracks, a formal one and a personal one. The formal one consists of the celebration of the Eucharist and praying the Liturgy of the Hours. The Liturgy of the Hours consists of psalms, a Scripture reading, some intercessions, and a concluding prayer. It's prayed four times a day, at morning, noon, evening, and night.

"My personal prayer is rather simple. I just slowly recite the Jesus Prayer for a while and then follow the silence that ensues. When I get distracted, I return to the Jesus Prayer. So my personal prayer is more like Centering Prayer."

"Centering Prayer?" Edward asked.

"Yes. Centering Prayer is a technique . . ."

"I know what Centering Prayer is, Father. I'm surprised you practice it. It's very dangerous and I don't think God approves of it. It's used in the pagan religions of the East and can open you to demonic influence. It's not found in the Bible. It's focused on yourself, not God, and is a form of self-hypnosis. It's designed to trick you into thinking you are experiencing God—but you're not! Do a google search and you'll discover all its dangers.

"You really should stick to the Psalms. I saw on the History Channel that Jesus used them when he prayed. Stick with them and the Lord's Prayer. God prefers them," Edward concluded.

A puny, picayune God restricts the divine presence to biblical forms of prayer.

Kristen's God

Phil and his wife were stunned when their friend Kristen told them she was not surprised that California's Caldor Fire had destroyed more than 221,000 acres and 670 structures in 2021. She matter-of-factly said, "That's God's way of letting those Californians know that their liberal laws are not acceptable. He's trying to wake them up."

A puny, picayune God is cruel and vindictive.

Scripture's God

A cursory look at Scripture, however, reveals a very different God—a big, bold, indomitable God, an omnipresent God, a magnificent and transcendent God. Here is a God who is not hindered or confined by time and space: God exists beyond the world of time (see Isa 40:28; Pss 90:1–4; 102:25–27). God transcends the limitations of space (see 1 Kgs 8:27; Jer 23:23–24; Ps 139:8–10). This is the Creator God whose power, wisdom, and understanding established the world and the heavens (see Jer 10:12; 32:17). God's thoughts are beyond human comprehension (see Isa 55:8–9). God's Spirit fills all creation and God's Wisdom orders all things (see Wis 1:7; 8:1). This God is "the Alpha and Omega" (Rev 1:8; 21:6), the source and goal of all creation.

The Book of Job

The utter magnificence of this big, bold God is on full display in the book of Job. In chapters 38 and 39, its author has God addressing Job out of a fierce storm. In the Old Testament, storms are often associated with God's appearances to humans (see Exod 19:16–20; 1 Kgs 19:11–13; Ps 8:7–17; Hab 3:14). As an aspect of revelation, the storm "implies a deity who is wild, beautiful, free, and deeply unsettling."[2]

Reading like lyric poetry, God asks Job question after question, each one proclaiming his creative magnificence:

- Where were you when I laid the foundation of the earth? (38:4)

- Have you entered into the springs of the sea, or walked in the recesses of the deep? (v. 16)

- Has the rain a father, or who has begotten the drops of dew? (v. 28)

- Can you send forth lightnings, so that they may go and say to you, "Here we are"? (v. 35)

These questions convey God's creativity in the creation of the cosmos. God attends not only to the vastness of the ocean and its depths but also to the details of dew and lightning. This is an

2. O'Connor, "The Book of Job," 521.

indomitable and unflinching God of majesty and power and splendor and glory.

God then goes on to emphasize the divine ingenuity in giving the animal world its habits and habitat:

- Do you know when the mountain goats give birth? Do you observe the calving of the deer? (39:1)

- Is the wild ox willing to serve you? Will it spend the night at your crib? (v. 9)

- Do you give the horse its might? Do you clothe its neck with mane? (v. 19)

- Is it by your wisdom that the hawk soars, and spreads its wings toward the south? (v. 26)

God highlights the variety, strength, and prowess of the animal kingdom, again indicating divine creativity, magnificence, and attention to details.

The Immanence of God

Paradoxically, this creative, magnificent, and transcendent God was not content to remain distant and detached but became deeply enmeshed in the activities of a small tribe of people. Transcendence gave way to immanence. God chose the Hebrew people as "his treasured people" (Deut 26:18) and made a covenant with Abraham (see Gen 17:1–2). God freed the chosen people from Egyptian slavery and continued the covenant with Moses (see Exod 19:3–6). God gave this treasured people their own country of Canaan (see Josh 1:11) and, continuing the covenant with David, established him as monarch (see 2 Sam 7:8–16). God offered counsel to the chosen people through the prophets (see 2 Kgs 17:13) and brought them back from captivity in Babylon (see Isa 40:1–2). God's immanent involvement eventually looked beyond this people to the salvation of all the world (see Isa 2:2–4; 45:22; Jer 16:19–20).

The salvation of the world would be accomplished not simply by divine power but by a divine person. Immanence included incarnation: not content to be involved with the chosen people simply through action, the transcendent God "became flesh and lived among us" (John 1:14). Jesus—"the image of the invisible God . . . in [whom] all the fullness of God was pleased to dwell" (Col 1:15, 19)—is the Son of God (see John 2:16; 5:18; Rom 15:6; Heb 1:1–2; 1 Pet 1:3) sent to accomplish God's salvific mission (see 2 Cor 5:19). God raised him from the dead, gave him a seat at his right hand in the heavenly places (see Eph 1:20), and gifted him with the Holy Spirit to be given to all believers (see Acts 2:33; John 7:39).

Such a history with us challenges any puny, picayune God such as Edward's and Kristen's. Indeed, this history portrays a big, bodacious God: a God who is beyond the universe and yet who carefully watches over the details of each saint and every sinner.

God of the Insignificant

Scientists tell us that our ever-expanding and still-evolving universe is approximately 14.7 billion years old. There are more than 100 billion galaxies. Our own galaxy, the Milky Way, is an intermediate-size galaxy consisting of 100 billion stars and stretching some 100,000 light years in diameter.[3] Our planet, one of at least 100 billion planets in our galaxy, is a grain of sand on the cosmic beach; 7.9 billion human beings reside on that grain of sand. When compared to the immensity of the cosmos, human beings are infinitesimally and statistically insignificant. The late theoretical physicist Stephen Hawking summed it up best in an interview with Ken Campbell in 1995 when he said, "The human race is just a chemical scum on a moderate-sized planet, orbiting around a very average star in the outer suburb of one among a hundred billion galaxies."[4]

3. Toolan, *At Home*, 132–55; Simon Singh, *Big Bang*, 144–61.

4. Spata, "7 Stephen Hawking Quotes," blog post, *Tampa Bay Times*.

Though the psalmist had no idea what was beyond his field of vision and did not know the universe as we now know it, he nevertheless gave voice to an indisputable question:

> When I look at your heavens, the work of your fingers,
>> the moon and the stars that you have established;
>> what are human beings that you are mindful of them,
>> mortals that you care for them? (Ps 8:3–4)

The psalmist wonders why God would be invested in individual men and women, trivial and trifling as they are when compared to the wonders of the midnight sky. The psalmist sings with awe, amazement, and wonder:

> Yet you have made them a little lower than God,
>> and crowned them with glory and honor.
> You have given them dominion over the works
> of your hands;
>> you have put all things under their feet,
> all sheep and oxen,
>> and also the beasts of the field,
> the birds of the air, and the fish of the sea,
>> whatever passes along the paths of the seas.
> O LORD, our Sovereign,
>> how majestic is your name in all the earth! (Ps 8:5–9)

What baffles the psalmist and sets his heart on fire with praise and adoration for God is the creation of humans with glory and honor. God has given humans dominion over creation and has provided everything they need in order to survive and thrive, including food stuffs, like sheep, oxen, birds, and fish. His is the Creator God of the universe who honors and ennobles even the most insignificant.

In Psalm 139, called by a Jewish scholar "one of the most remarkably introspective psalms in the canonical collection,"[5] the

---

5. Alter, *The Book of Psalms*, 479.

psalmist celebrates God's personal investment and knowledge of his human insignificance. God knows when the psalmist sits and rises (Ps 139:2), is acquainted with all his ways (v. 3), and even knows the words on his tongue before the psalmist speaks them (v. 4). Awed by such divine investment and knowledge, the psalmist sings, "Such knowledge is too wonderful for me" (v. 6).

This Creator God of the universe is also inescapable. God is present in the heavens and in the depths of Sheol (v. 8). If the psalmist travels from the rising of the sun in the east to its setting in the west, God's hand leads him and holds him safe (v. 9). Not even the cover of darkness can hide the psalmist from the divine presence (v. 11–12).

Suddenly, the psalmist has a flash of an insight into why God knows him so well and is invested in him:

> For it was you who formed my inward parts;
>> you knit me together in my mother's womb.
> I praise you, for I am fearfully and wonderfully made.
>> Wonderful are your works;
>> that I know very well.
> My frame was not hidden from you,
>> when I was being made in secret,
>> intricately woven in the depths of the earth.
> Your eyes beheld my unformed substance.
>> In your book were written
>> all the days that were formed for me,
>> when none of them as yet existed. (Ps 139:13–16)

God deliberately and intentionally created the psalmist, a single human being among billions of others residing on that grain of sand that is the earth. God knows this individual through and through and is actively conscious of his every word and action. Like a sculptor, God "beheld" him even before he was formed. Like a craftsman, God formed his "inmost parts," the literal meaning of the Hebrew is "kidneys."[6] Like a weaver, God created his body, knitting bones and sinews into an artistic creation. The eyes of the divine are fixed on what would become the days and years of his lifetime. His is the Creator God of the universe who honors even the smallest details—down to the kidneys—of the most insignificant creature, one of 7.9 billion human beings. The wonders of nature and his own creation make the psalmist aware of God's investment in the insignificant affairs of a human person.

The Teaching of Jesus

Like the psalmist, Jesus himself looked to the wonders of nature to highlight God's investment in human affairs. His well-known teaching is as eloquent as it is challenging:

> Consider the ravens: they neither sow nor reap, they have neither storehouse nor barn, and yet God feeds them. Of how much more value are you than the birds! . . . Consider the lilies, how they grow: they neither toil nor spin; yet I tell you, even Solomon in all his glory was not clothed like one of these. But if God so clothes the grass of the field, which is alive today and tomorrow is thrown into the oven, how much more will he clothe you—you of little faith! (Luke 12:24, 27–28)

Two examples from nature allow Jesus to once again employ the rabbinical technique called *qal wehomer*, a process of deduction where something that applies in a lesser case must also apply in a more important one. It accentuates his message about God's care and concern.

The Greek word *korax*, translated as "ravens," can also be translated as "crows." Both birds are scavengers. Jews were forbidden to eat such animals and gentile Greeks considered them disgusting. If God cares for a repulsive carrion eater, how much

6. Alter, *The Book of Psalms*, 481.

more will God be invested in human beings made in the divine image and likeness?[7]

Jesus repeats the point with reference to the *krinon*, translated here as "lilies" though probably meaning "crocus" or "rose of Sharon" (see Song 2:1). During the Galilean rainy season, these flowers would be stunning against the green hillsides. But as soon as the temperature rose, they would shrivel up. They then would be harvested and used as fuel in ovens. "If God shows so much attention to what ends up in the fire, how much more does he care for his people."[8]

Encouraging his followers to be faithful even in the midst of persecution, Jesus again looks to nature for justification. "Are not five sparrows sold for two pennies? Yet not one of them is forgotten in God's sight. But even the hairs of your head are all counted" (Luke 12:6–7). God's care and concern are focused on the apparently mundane and the seemingly insignificant, down to a strand of hair.

The Little Way

Living with the awareness of God's rapt attention to the smallest detail of her life was one aspect of the spirituality of the nineteenth-century Saint Thérèse of Lisieux.

Thérèse spent the last decade of her life behind the walls of a cloistered Carmelite monastery in France. She died in 1897 of tuberculosis at the age of twenty-four. She lived her life in the monastery practicing what she called "the little way" or "the way of spiritual childhood."

Recognizing her eminent understanding of the spiritual life and her great sanctity, Pope John Paul II on October 19, 1997, conferred upon her the honorific title of Doctor of the Church. At the time, she was only the third woman to receive this honor.

---

7. Patella, "The Gospel according to Luke," 1136–37.
8. Patella, "The Gospel according to Luke," 1137.

In his homily conferring this honorific title on Saint Thérèse, Pope John Paul II noted the saint's sensitivity to God's attention. He said:

> [Thérèse] counters a rational culture, so often overcome by practical materialism, with the disarming simplicity of the "little way" which, by returning to the essentials, leads to the secret of all life: the divine Love that surrounds and penetrates every human venture.[9]

Like a loving, vigilant, and conscientious parent, God's care and concern are fixated on every single human undertaking and endeavor, both great and small: mending a button on a shirt, washing dishes, feeding the family pet, sticking one's toes in the sand of a beach, looking for employment, raising a child, burying a loved one. Nothing is excluded from God's interest and attentiveness. This is "the secret of all life," to quote Pope John Paul II.

Though she never quoted Jesus' saying, "Truly I tell you, unless you change and become like children, you will never enter the kingdom of heaven" (Matt 18:3), Thérèse clearly saw that she must foster and maintain childlike trust in a loving Father who was intent in caring for every aspect of her life. When asked to explain the way of spiritual childhood in the final year of her life, this Doctor of the Church replied:

> It means that we acknowledge our nothingness, that we expect everything from the good Lord, as a child expects everything from its father; it means to worry about nothing, not to build on fortune; it means to remain little. . . . It means that we must not be discouraged by our faults, for children fall frequently.[10]

Her holiness was rooted in a stance of humility before a God who not only was invested in everything about her but also could be trusted to respond to the most insignificant details of her day. In one of the final conversations she had before she died,

9. As cited in St. Thérèse of Lisieux, *The Story of a Soul*, v–vi.

10. As cited in Jamart, *Complete Spiritual Doctrine*, 15–16.

Thérèse famously said, "Everything is a grace because everything is God's gift."[11]

Ours is a bold, indomitable, unflinching God. A big, bodacious God. A God of infinite power and abiding presence. A God beyond the limitations of space and time. A transcendent God who is the creator of 100 billion galaxies, black holes, quasars, and supernovas. A God of the sea, the rain, and the lightning. A God who notices a mountain goat, a deer, a wild ox, a horse, and a hawk. A God who counts every strand of hair. And yet, paradoxically, a God who took notice of the affairs and activities of a small tribe of people and established a covenant with them. A God who joined 7.9 billion human beings living on a cosmic grain of sand and became enmeshed and involved with the details of their lives. A God who walked dusty roads and washed feet. This unimaginable, transcendent, gift-giving God is so mysterious and so entangled in the small stuff of the human experience that divine care and concern include fixing a borrowed, broken axe and finding Patrick's favorite jacket.

11. Schmidt, *Everything Is Grace*, 302.

Reflect

How big is my God? Is my God interested in helping me find a spouse? A parking spot? Just the right birthday gift for a friend? A lost set of keys?

Practice

Google "list of patron saints by occupation and activity" and "patron saints of ailments, illness, and danger." Spend time reading the lists for fun. Then reflect how both lists show just how invested God is in your everyday worries, concerns, and challenges. Spend time journaling your reflections and any surprising insights you may have gained.

Ponder

> On one occasion our good Lord said, "All things will be well," on another, "You will see for yourself that all manner of things will be well." In both these statements we can see different levels of meaning. One was this: that Christ wants us to know that he takes care not only of the noble and great things but also of the humble and small, lowly and simple things—all are equal. That is what he means by "All manner of things will be well." He wants us to know that the least thing will not be forgotten.
>
> —Julian of Norwich[12]

Pray

You boggle my mind, O loving and mysterious Creator. Out of your infinite wisdom and generosity, you have created a universe that thrills me with wonder and awe. And yet, at the same time, I am baffled that you care enough to minister to my meager worries and insignificant concerns. May I never forget that your care and

12. Julian of Norwich, *Revelations*, 92.

concern reach all the way down to my stubbed toe. I ask this in the name of Jesus the Lord. Amen.

8

Open Your Eyes

2 Kings 6:8–19

AT THE END OF February 1944, fifty-one-year-old Corrie ten Boom and her sister Betsie were arrested and imprisoned in Scheveningen Prison for their involvement in the Dutch underground resistance network that included harboring Jews in their home and smuggling them to safe places. Within four months, both were transferred to the notorious Ravensbrück concentration camp, built exclusively for women, in northern Germany. They were initially assigned to Barracks 8 and then permanently moved to Barracks 28 with its broken windows stuffed with rags and a putrefying smell from the stench of reeking straw used for bedding. Besides the overall squalor of this overcrowded barracks and the unimaginable horror of living in a concentration camp, Barracks 28 had another problem.

Within an hour of settling in to the new barracks, Corrie discovered it.

"Fleas!" Corrie exclaimed. "Betsie, the place is swarming with them. . . . How can we live in such a place?"

Corrie heard Betsie mumble, "Show us. Show us how."

At first not understanding what she meant, Corrie suddenly realized that her older sister was praying and asking God to give them the eyes to see how they could manage such conditions.

Continuing to pray, Betsie then exclaimed, "He's given us the answer! Before we asked, as He always does! In the Bible this morning. Where was it? Read that part again!"

Corrie surreptitiously pulled out the Bible that had slipped by the guards when they arrived at the camp. She read again the passage from that morning's devotional time:

> And we urge you, beloved, to admonish the idlers, encourage the fainthearted, help the weak, be patient with all of them. See that none of you repays evil for evil, but always seek to do good to one another and to all. Rejoice always, pray without ceasing, give thanks in all circumstances; for this is the will of God in Christ Jesus for you.
> (1 Thess 5:14–18)

Betsie exclaimed, "That's it, Corrie! That's His answer. 'Give thanks in all circumstances.' That's what we can do. We can start right now to thank God for every single thing about our new barracks."

Corrie wasn't convinced.

Betsie explained that the two sisters had not been separated and were still together. They had the Bible. And they had the opportunity to share the Word of God with their fellow inmates.

"But the fleas," Corrie interrupted her sister, "Betsie, there's no way even God can make me thankful for a flea."

Corrie soon would regret those words.

Betsie and Corrie held simple worship services in the back of their barracks. As the number of worshipers increased, the two sisters feared discovery by the prison guards. And yet, they were baffled by the lack of supervision inside the barracks.

That bewilderment soon turned into gratitude for the fleas.

One evening, Betsie related to Corrie an incident that had occurred earlier in the day. That afternoon, Betsie and some prisoners were doing their work assignment of knitting socks for the German soldiers. A question arose about sock size. The prisoners asked for the supervisor to come and answer the question.

Both the supervisor and the prison guards refused to enter the barracks. Betsie explained their reluctance to her younger sister. "Because of the fleas! That's what the supervisor said: 'That place is crawling with fleas!'"[1]

Both sisters' eyes of faith were opened. They could "rejoice" and "give thanks" even for the fleas because God, using those small wingless bloodsucking insects as instruments of his grace and protection, was acting and moving among them. Because of those fleas, Corrie and Betsie were able to preach the Word of God and convert many inmates to Christ.

Surrounded by the Enemy

Like Corrie and Betsie, one of Elisha's attendants also had his eyes of faith opened and saw God's grace and protection amid a difficult situation.

While at war with Israel, the king of Aram took counsel with his officers. He decided where he would pitch his camp for the next attack.

Elisha informed the king of Israel where the Arameans would be, thus allowing the army of Israel to be on the alert.

After having his attacks thwarted a couple of times, the king of Aram began to suspect a traitor among his officers. He called a meeting to expose him.

During the meeting, his officers informed the king that there was no traitor among them. One of the officers said, "It is Elisha, the prophet in Israel, who tells the king of Israel the words that you speak in your bedchamber" (2 Kgs 6:12).

The king demanded that Elisha be captured. Learning that the man of God was in the city of Dothan, the king sent "horses and chariots there and a great army" (v. 14) and surrounded the city at night.

When one of Elisha's attendants rose early in the morning and discovered the army surrounding the city, he exclaimed, "Alas, master! What shall we do?" (v. 15). He no doubt realized their inability to defeat or escape the might of the king of Aram.

1. Ten Boom, *The Hiding Place*, 180–81, 189–90.

Aware of God's grace and protection, the man of God told his attendant, "Do not be afraid, for there are more with us than there are with them" (v. 16). Elisha prayed, "'O Lord, please open his eyes that he may see.' So the Lord opened the eyes of the servant, and he saw; the mountain was full of horses and chariots of fire all around Elisha" (v. 17). A favorable army was protecting them from the Aramean army.

At first, the attendant could only see the enemy. But in answer to the prophet's prayer, his eyes of faith were opened, and he saw divine grace and protection amid a desperate and precarious situation. God was close by, moving and working in their midst just as God would do later in Barracks 28 of Ravensbrück.

Was this an angelic army that miraculously appeared? Had the king of Israel been informed of the Aramean presence in Dothan and sent his army under cover of night? The text is not clear. All we know is that Elisha and his attendants were aware of the presence and protection of God.

When the attack on Elisha and his men began, Elisha prayed that God would strike the Arameans with blindness. God responded to his prayer and the enemy was blinded. Elisha then lied to the Arameans, "This is not the way, and this is not the city; follow me, and I will bring you to the man whom you seek" (v. 19). He then led the enemy to Samaria.

The Mount of Olives

In the last hours of his life, Jesus himself would not be exempt from a desperate and difficult situation. Nor would he be exempt from God's presence and protection. Luke's account includes a curious detail.

Having celebrated the Passover with his disciples, Jesus walked out to the Mount of Olives "as was his custom" (Luke 22:39; 21:37). Telling his attendant disciples, "Pray that you may not come into the time of trial" (22:40), he withdrew from them, knelt down, and prayed, "Father, if you are willing, remove this cup from me; yet, not my will but yours be done" (v. 42).

Some ancient manuscripts, not all, continue, "Then an angel from heaven appeared to him and gave him strength" (v. 43).

The Greek *ángelos*, translated here as "angel," literally means "messenger." Who was this messenger from heaven who ministered to Jesus and gave him the fortitude and courage to face his impending death? An unnamed traveler who happened upon Jesus in prayer? A disciple who had followed him to his place of prayer? A heavenly visitor or spiritual being? The text does not say—but clearly the evangelist wants the reader to know that in his time of trial, God's grace and protection were present to Jesus. And the positive effect of that ministering messenger is evident as Luke, unlike Matthew and Mark (see Matt 26:37; Mark 14:34), removes any mention of Jesus' grief, considered a character flaw in Greco-Roman culture,[2] and instead applies it to the disciples "sleeping because of grief" (v. 45).

The Death of Jesus

God's grace and protection were not just present to Jesus on the Mount of Olives. They also were present on Calvary.

Many readers of the Gospels of Matthew and Mark are taken aback by Jesus' apparent distress and despair at the time of his death. Both accounts quote Jesus in a mixture of Hebrew and his native Aramaic, "Eli, Eli, lema sabachthani?" and then translate the words for the reader, "My God, my God, why have you forsaken me?" (Matt 27:46; Mark 15:34). These words, the beginning of Psalm 22, could give the reader the impression that Jesus felt forsaken and forlorn. But that is not the whole story. As one biblical scholar aptly notes:

> The words here constitute the opening of Psalm 22, and
> their significance increases if one knows the whole psalm.
> It is a psalm in which the speaker begins in despair and
> moves to an encounter with death, but then is rescued
> by God, and concludes with thanksgiving and praise. If
> one knows the whole structure, then the opening verse

2. Hamm, "Luke," 1096.

recalls not only the speaker's initial agony but also his eventual rescue and restoration.[3]

The psalmist sings Psalm 22 with wide-open eyes: the psalmist refuses to sugarcoat or repress raw, excruciating emotions. In three separate complaint sections of this lament psalm, the psalmist lays bare graphic feelings: In the first section, the psalmist expresses the feeling of abandonment by a God who does not respond to the cries for help (vv. 1–2). In the second section, the psalmist expresses feelings of worthlessness as the psalmist is scorned, despised, and mocked by others (vv. 6–8). In the third complaint section, the psalmist expresses feelings of weakness and helplessness against enemies who are compared to "bulls" and "dogs" (vv. 12–18).

Amid these feelings of abandonment, worthlessness, weakness, and helplessness, the psalmist also expresses a confidence in divine grace and protection. Indeed, his wide-open eyes are eyes of faith: in response to the first complaint of feeling abandoned, the psalmist reminds God that "our ancestors" trusted in divine help and were not disappointed (vv. 3–5). In response to the complaint of feeling worthless, the psalmist compares God to a midwife who protected the psalmist "on my mother's breast" and was the deity worshiped from the first day of the psalmist's life (vv. 9–11). Responding to the third complaint with a plea for divine help (vv. 9–21), the psalmist bursts into a prayer of praise and thanksgiving for a God who responds with grace and protection (vv. 21–31). That divine response to the psalmist will not be forgotten:

> Posterity will serve him;
>> future generations will be told about the Lord,
> and proclaim his deliverance to a people yet unborn,
>> saying that he has done it. (v. 30–31)

By praying Psalm 22 from the cross, Jesus was showing that even in the last moments of his life, his eyes of faith were wide open. His pain became praise, and his suffering became song: like Elisha's attendant, he gave voice not only to his desperation and

3. Sabin, "The Gospel according to Mark," 1097.

distress but also, like Elisha, proclaimed trust and confidence in his Father's grace and protection. Indeed, just as would happen later in Barracks 28 of Ravensbrück, God was moving in and around an apparently hopeless situation.

The Abiding Presence of God

One of the central tenets of Christian spirituality is the abiding presence of God—everywhere, in all situations, and at all times, both good and bad. Our challenge is to open our eyes of faith and discover this divine presence.

This is a major pillar of the spirituality of sixteenth-century Ignatius of Loyola. When National Public Radio's Krista Tippett asked Fr. James Martin, SJ, to describe the distinctive characteristic of Ignatian spirituality, the famous Jesuit priest and author replied:

> Probably the shortest way of describing it is finding God in all things. And the idea is that God is not simply to be found in our prayer life, which is very important, or in worship services and Mass or in reading the Bible. All those are important and at the center of that kind of spirituality. But in your daily life, in your relationships, in your work, in the emotions that come up, in those moments that you see a sunset and you say, "My gosh that's so beautiful. Why am I feeling like this?" Or you see an infant for the first time, like your niece or your nephew . . . and you say, "My gosh, where are these feelings coming from?" And these are ways that God has of communicating with us through our daily lives in all things.[4]

Elisha's prayer on behalf of his attendant, "O Lord, please open his eyes that he may see," is the prayer we should pray daily for ourselves so we can see God in the people who cross our paths, the situations in which we find ourselves, our deepest feelings, and our most creative thoughts. Having the wide-open eyes of faith is finding God and divine messengers in all things.

4. Martin, "James Martin: Finding God in All Things."

Of course, as the old adage says, it's easier said than done. Our senses sometimes make us incapable of seeing God and divine messengers in the midst of darkness. Emotions such as grief, fear, anger, betrayal, intimidation, loneliness, and powerlessness have a way of blinding us. But the eyes of faith do not depend upon our five senses. Those eyes, like night vision goggles, see through the darkness. Another Jesuit, the twentieth-century French priest, scientist, and philosopher Pierre Teilhard de Chardin, SJ, hints that the abiding presence of God can be found even in the darkness of death: "In the shadow of death may we not look back to the past, but seek in utter darkness the dawn of God."[5] Elisha, Jesus, and Corrie ten Boom certainly would resonate with those words.

Rita's Pigeon

And so would Albert's mother. Albert vividly remembers an experience when he suddenly realized that his mother had learned to live with the wide-open eyes of faith, seeing God's presence and protection in all things and at all times.

His mother became a widow at age forty-two. Three of her five children, Albert being the youngest, were still at home and needed to finish their high school and college educations. Having been a stay-at-home mother with only a high school education, his mother had no professional skills to enter the workforce. A debt of $60,000 incurred by Albert's father before he died by suicide exacerbated the financial challenges. The house and automobile had to be sold and the family moved in with Albert's maternal grandmother.

Within a few months after the funeral and the sale of the house, Albert's mother took copies of her thin résumé and would stand at the corner of Fountainbleau Drive and South Salcedo, waiting for the Broad-Lowerline bus. She would get on that bus and take it to Canal Street where she would transfer to the Canal Street streetcar that brought her to the business district of New

5. Cited in Harter, *Hearts on Fire*, 73.

Orleans. Once there, she would pound the pavement, visit job site after job site, and pass out her simple résumé. This went on for weeks with no job offers.

Albert's mother loved to tell her children the story about the pigeon. The details never changed.

"One day, I was so worried and depressed about having little success with my job hunt. I stood on the street corner, again waiting for the Broad-Lowerline bus. 'Oh Lord,' I prayed, 'I just don't know what to do. How am I going to support my children? I am desperate for a job.'

"Suddenly, a pigeon walked across my right foot. I looked down at it and suddenly heard a voice in my heart say, 'Rita, look at the birds of the air. I take care of them. I'll take care of you and your family.'"

Seeds of trust and confidence were planted in her heart. As the Christmas holidays approached, Albert's mother began telling her children, "We'll get through all of this. God has promised that he'll take care of us."

Months turned to years. Albert's two oldest brothers finished their education, married, and had children. Albert went to the seminary, entered the Franciscan Order, was ordained a Catholic priest, and fulfilled his childhood dream of being a missionary among the Chinese people. And the boys' mother? She went to a business school, received some computer skills, and was hired and ultimately retired as a computer specialist for a large national insurance company.

Thirty-seven years after his mother's encounter with the pigeon, Albert returned from eleven years of missionary activity in mainland China. At this point, Albert's mother had been suffering from Alzheimer's disease for more than six years and was a resident in an Alzheimer's unit in Waterville, Maine. One of Albert's priorities after returning to the States was to visit his mother.

He flew to Maine and made his way to the nursing home. "Hello, I'm here to see my mother, Rita Haase," he told the receptionist at the front desk.

"Oh, you mean, *Miss* Rita. That's how we address her. She's such a sweet, southern lady. Let me call Louise. She's your mother's attending nurse." After meeting Albert and exchanging some basic information, Louise led Albert to his mother's bedroom.

"Miss Rita has her good days and her bad days. So you'll need to be prepared. She spends a lot of time asleep and, if she does wake up, she might not recognize you. That's what this terrible disease does. It just robs people of their memories."

Arriving in the room, Louise said, "Miss Rita, I bring you tidings of great joy! You have a special visitor."

Albert's mother momentarily opened her eyes and then closed them. "This might be a good day," Louise whispered to Albert.

With a heavy sigh over just three annual phone calls, on Christmas, her birthday, and Mother's Day, Albert took a deep breath and tried to muster up some grit. He looked around the room and saw the framed picture of him and his four siblings hanging on the wall. Next to the bed, he saw his mother's prayer books and Bible.

Memories rushed into consciousness. Albert remembered how his mother read daily prayers from those books. And she loved her Bible. "It's my plane ticket to heaven," she often said.

Pulling up a chair and sitting next to her bed, Albert took her by the hand and said, "Mama, it's me. Your youngest son. Albert."

His mother opened her eyes and tilted her head slightly to the right. Albert thought he saw a twinkle of recognition. And maybe an attempt at a smile. But his mother quickly closed her eyes again.

Not wanting to lose what he hoped would be a special moment on a good day, Albert searched for something to say. He picked up his mother's Bible—that "plane ticket to heaven"—and flipped through it. He was suddenly puzzled and confused. The Bible was in pristine condition. Some pages still stuck together like new books do and the binding even cracked a bit. *This can't be her Bible,* he thought. He looked at it again. Apparently, it *was* her Bible. *How could it be in such good condition?* As he flipped through it, he suddenly came to the Gospel of Matthew. He noticed a passage underlined in blue ink, highlighted with a yellow marker, and oil-stained, no doubt from the Jergens lotion his mother had used each evening on her hands. The passage was from the Sermon on the Mount:

> Therefore I tell you, do not worry about your life, what you will eat or what you will drink, or about your body, what you will wear. Is not life more than food, and the body more than clothing? Look at the birds of the air; they neither sow nor reap nor gather into barns, and yet your heavenly Father feeds them. Are you not of more value than they? (Matt 6:25–26)

Trying to make a little joke, Albert chuckled and said, "Mama, I can't believe it. I always remember you saying your prayers and reading your Bible. But I'm holding your Bible in my hands right now, and it's very clear to me that you haven't really read it. All you seem to have read are two verses."

A silence descended.

Suddenly, Albert's mother opened her eyes. Tilting her head to the right and grasping for words in the slow, halting voice of an Alzheimer's patient, his mother whispered, "You . . . Big, fancy . . . degree in theology. . . . Only . . . one thing . . . is . . . important . . . to know . . . and . . . remember. Look at . . . the . . . birds . . . of . . . the . . . air." And with that, the dark, heavy clouds of Alzheimer's disease moved in again and her eyes closed.

Albert's mother's encounter with the pigeon in New Orleans was an eye-opening event. It made her see with the eyes of faith that God's grace and protection were working in the very midst of her family's tragedy and her struggles for employment. Not even Alzheimer's disease could rob her of that memory.

Fr. Bill Atkinson, OSA

Nor could a life-changing accident—for Bill Atkinson.

Born within the first week of 1946 in Philadelphia, Bill Atkinson would spend sixty years with his eyes wide open. At the age of eighteen, he entered the Order of Saint Augustine, commonly called the Augustinians. He had dreams of studying for the priesthood.

His life took a drastic and dramatic turn on February 22, 1965. On that cold afternoon in western New York, his toboggan hit a tree. He broke his spine and was left completely paralyzed from the neck down, with limited movement of his head, neck, shoulders, and arms. He would spend the rest of his life in a motorized wheelchair.

As a quadriplegic, it was doubtful if he could ever minister as a priest. But Bill continued to feel called to the priesthood. By a special dispensation personally signed by Pope Paul VI, Bill was ordained on February 2, 1974. He was the first quadriplegic ever ordained to the priesthood in the two-thousand-year history of the Roman Catholic Church.

For almost thirty years, he was involved in ministry as a high school theology teacher, assistant school chaplain, senior class retreat moderator, and moderator of the football team.

An inspiration to all who met him, Fr. Bill was known for his wonderful smile and sense of humor. And his profound belief that God could be found in the smallest details of his life. Albert remembers him telling the story about the day he had an itchy nose. "I prayed and prayed and it took two hours for God to send someone to scratch it!"

Fr. Bill Atkinson lived his life in utter trust of God's grace and protection—with the wide-open eyes of faith. He died on September 15, 2006. Nine years later, his Cause for Canonization as a saint in the Roman Catholic Church was formally opened.

The Eyes of Faith

You don't have to be on the formal road to sainthood to have your vision validated.

Jeremy knows well Jesus' experience of being ministered to by a heavenly messenger. When his wife of thirty-five years died, family and friends rallied around him. They gave him listening ears, shoulders to cry on, and brought him prepared meals for several months. "I never would have been able to get through my grief without their help—and I thought for sure I would never be able to handle life without Sarah. But the support of my family and friends gave me the courage to ease into and manage living alone. They were reminders that God continues to care for me each and every day." Jeremy found God even in the midst of his wife's death.

When he was serving as pastor, a member of Phil's church suggested that Sherry schedule an appointment with him. For forty years, Sherry was known among family and friends as "the Stunning Soprano" and often gave benefit concerts to raise funds for needy causes. When her voice began to crack on occasion, she suspected something wasn't quite right.

"After seeing a few specialists," she told Phil, "I was diagnosed with ALS, commonly called Lou Gehrig's disease. The doctor told me that I would gradually lose my voice."

A year later, Sherry again sat in Phil's office. When Phil asked her how she was doing, she typed her response on a speech-generating device and pressed Read. "I'm doing fine."

"Sherry, I so admire you. I just don't know how you can manage this challenge with such faith and grace."

"Pastor Phil," the speech-generating device replied, "I once heard someone say: 'When everything falls apart, fall into the arms of God, and trust he knows what he's doing.'"

At that very moment, Phil's eyes were opened as he realized that Sherry's pain had become praise. Her suffering became song as she surrendered to ALS and trusted God would stay near to her. She was an incarnation of Psalm 22.

The Prayer of Remembrance

Living with the wide-open eyes of faith can be a challenge. A diagnosis of terminal cancer, a debt collector's pressuring phone call for funds one doesn't have, the loss of a job, the end of a treasured relationship, the experience of abuse, a spousal betrayal, and other myriad experiences can shatter one's belief and trust in God's grace and protection. Is there a way to keep the eyes of faith open?

The Prayer of Remembrance is a simple technique that can help open your eyes to see God's presence and protection at all times and in all things. It's based upon seven Rs and ideally is practiced once a year. You should allow as much time as needed—don't rush through it. Some people like to include it in their journal. It's an ideal exercise for a weekend retreat or day of personal prayer and reflection.

Request

Begin the Prayer of Remembrance by calling upon the help of the Holy Spirit to open your eyes, your ears, and your heart to the presence of God. This can be as simple as "Come, Holy Spirit, and heal me of my blindness, deafness, and hard-heartedness so that I may experience the divine presence in all the experiences of my life."

Review

Carefully look over your entire life. Start with your earliest memory. Walk through your childhood, adolescence, and adulthood. Note your disappointments, challenges, and tragedies. Try to remember and reexperience the frustration, hurt, pain, and suffering that arose from them. Don't forget to spend time with the sins you still remember and bitterly regret.

Reflect

Consider this question: how did these challenges and sins affect me? Ask three further questions:

- What did these challenges and sins say to my head? What information did they convey about God's relationship with me?

- What did these challenges and sins say to my heart? What emotions did they elicit?

- What did these challenges and sins say to my hands? How did I respond to them?

Mull over how God's grace and protection were present to you in your talents and abilities, your family and friends, and the subsequent situations and circumstances that arose as consequences to those challenges and sins. Who was the heavenly messenger sent to minister to you?

When contemplating your sins, don't forget the wisdom of Saint Paul: "where sin increased, grace abounded all the more" (Rom 5:20).

Remember

Write down or commit to memory what you learned about God's presence in your times of trials and sinfulness. This can prove worthwhile, helpful, and encouraging when future challenges and trials come your way and you are tempted to lose hope. It can also be helpful when you are discouraged by your sins.

Resolve

Make the commitment to put your trust in God's abiding presence at all times and in all things. This is not a feeling but an act of the will. It often begins in the head and ever so gradually makes its way to the heart. This is what it means to live with the wide-open eyes of faith.

Rejoice

Conclude with a prayer of praise and thanksgiving to God for being present to you in your times of need, trial, and sinfulness. You might want to write your own prayer in the spirit of Psalm 22 or Mary's Magnificat (Luke 1:46–55).

Revisit

Two or three times a year, return to your notes and reread the history of God's grace and protection in your life. This will help sensitize you to the abiding presence of the divine.

Amid coping with fleas, surrounded by an army, struggling to accept an apparent trial, feeling abandoned, looking for employment, accepting an accident that leaves you a quadriplegic, or living with a disease, we are challenged to "give thanks in all circumstances" (1 Thess 5:18). The Prayer of Remembrance gives us insight into why we personally should offer praise and thanks to God in every situation. Like Elisha, we keep our eyes open, fully aware that divine grace and protection are working in every circumstance in which we find ourselves. In doing so, "we walk by faith, not by sight" (2 Cor 5:7).

Reflect

What was the most difficult trial or tragedy I have ever experienced? How did God minister to me during it? At the time, how aware was I of God's grace and protection?

Practice

Spend a morning or afternoon with the seven Rs of the Prayer of Remembrance. Within a week, look over what you have discovered and assess the usefulness of the Prayer of Remembrance for you.

Ponder

> A person "should become a God-seeker in all things and a God-finder at all times, in all places, in all company, in all ways."[6]
>
> —Meister Eckhart

Pray

Jesus, you did not hesitate to give voice to your fears and feelings as you prayed on the Mount of Olives and hung upon the cross on Calvary. As the darkness of death approached, you kept your eyes open to the grace and protection of your Father. And you were not disappointed. May I keep my eyes open when trials encircle me and with your help maintain my trust and confidence in divine assistance. In your Name, I pray. Amen.

6. Eckhart, *The Talks of Instruction*, #22, 516.

9 ___________________________________

Feed the Enemy

2 Kings 6:20–23

On February 12, 1993, a friend telephoned Mary Johnson at work. She asked if Mary's twenty-year-old son, Laramiun Byrd, had gotten home.

Mary asked the reason for the question. Her friend replied that she'd heard that his body was at the morgue.

Mary contacted her sister who called the police department.

When her sister called back, she said, "Mary, they said they're coming to see you, so it must be true."

Mary fainted. When she regained consciousness, her supervisor was holding her. She doesn't remember taking the short ride downtown, but by the time she arrived at her sister's house, Laramiun's body had been identified. Her son had been murdered in an argument at a North Minneapolis party.

Three days later, the police arrested sixteen-year-old Marlon Green and charged him with the first-degree murder of Laramiun Byrd.

"I believe hate set in then and there. Here was I, a Christian woman, full of hatred," Mary recalls.

Mary's anger increased when the judge suddenly changed the charge to the lesser offense of second-degree murder.

During the trial, Mary kept looking at Green. "I was full of hatred. I saw him as an animal. I wanted him caged. I wanted him locked up for the rest of his life. That was justice for me."

Mary looked forward to giving her victim-impact statement. "I was inspired by my faith, and so I ended off by saying I'd forgiven Marlon Green 'because the Bible tells us to forgive.'"

"But I hadn't actually forgiven," Mary says and continues, "The root of bitterness ran deep, anger had set in, and I hated everyone. I remained like this for years, driving many people away." She had no intention of forgiving her son's murderer.

Marlon Green, on the other hand, struggled with the guilt of murdering someone as he served his twenty-five-and-a-half-year sentence at the Minnesota Stillwater state prison. In an effort "to make a new beginning," Marlon Green changed his name to Oshea Israel.

One day, a book Mary was reading fell open to a poem entitled "Two Mothers." It was about two "angels" who meet in heaven and reminisce over the love they each had for their sons. At the end of the poem, the identities of the two mothers are revealed: one is Mary, the mother of Jesus, and the other is the mother of Judas Iscariot.[1]

After reading and reflecting on the poem, Mary felt the Holy Spirit speaking to her. "I want the mothers of murdered children and the mothers of children who took a life to get together and heal."

Mary's response? "And I said, 'Nope. Can't do this.'"

She soon got the idea, however, to found an organization that would become "From Death to Life." Since 2005, it has supported not only the mothers of murdered children but also the mothers of children who have taken a life.

Mary knew she had to really forgive Oshea if the organization was going to be what it was meant to be. "So I put in a request to the Department of Corrections to meet him," she remembers. Oshea turned down the initial request but agreed to the second request made nine months later.

Arriving at Stillwater for her first-ever prison visit, Mary was scared and began having second doubts about meeting her son's murderer. Oshea came into the room and the two shook hands.

1. Sykes, "Two Mothers."

"'I don't know you and you don't know me,'" Oshea remembers Mary saying. "'You didn't know my son and he didn't know you, so we need to lay down a foundation and get to know one another.'"

They talked for two hours with Oshea confessing to the murder. Mary could see his guilt and remorse. And for the first time, she was genuinely able to forgive Oshea. As the meeting ended, Mary told Oshea, "I forgive you from the bottom of my heart."

Oshea was skeptical. "Ma'am, how can you do that?"

Overcome with emotion, Mary broke down and seemed to melt into the floor. Oshea couldn't let her fall, so he hugged her as if she was his own mother.

A security guard quickly stepped in and returned Oshea to his cell.

As she left Stillwater, Mary recalls, "I felt something rising from the soles of my feet and leaving me. From that day on, I haven't felt any hatred, animosity, or anger. It was over."

Mary returned to Stillwater often. Mother and murderer talked about grace, forgiveness, and reconciliation.

In March 2010, after serving seventeen years of his sentence, Oshea was released from prison. Mary, some members of From Death to Life, and some Catholic nuns in the neighborhood organized a welcome home party and a sit-down meal.[2]

Food for the Enemy

Mary's meal celebrated both the grace of forgiveness and Oshea's release from prison. A different kind of meal, however, played an important role in de-escalating the animosity between Elisha and the Arameans.

Remember how the king of Aram had sent soldiers to Dothan to capture Elisha? And how God surrounded Elisha and his attendants with an army? And how Elisha prayed that the

2. "The Story of Mary Johnson," WonderingEagle blog, and "Mary Johnson and Oshea Israel," The Forgiveness Project blog.

Arameans be blinded and then lied, saying he would bring them to the place where the prophet resided?

Elisha led the blind and confused Arameans to the king of Israel in Samaria. When they arrived, Elisha prayed for God to open their eyes, allowing the Arameans to see that they had been tricked and were now surrounded by the Israelite army.

The king of Israel asked Elisha if he should kill them. Elisha responded, "No! Did you capture with your sword and your bow those whom you want to kill? Set food and water before them so that they may eat and drink; and let them go to their master" (2 Kgs 6:22).

The king of Israel prepared a great feast and afterward, allowed them to go free! The story ends with an important note, "And the Arameans no longer came raiding into the land of Israel" (v. 23).

Unlike Mary's celebratory meal that included the grace of forgiveness, Elisha's meal was based on a deliberate decision: respond to aggression with mercy. There is no mention of forgiveness. Since meals in ancient Israel were cultural celebrations of friendship and mutual obligation between the parties who partook of them, the result was a double blessing: for the Arameans, it meant life; for the Israelites, it meant an end to enemy hostilities.

The Nature of Forgiveness

Forgiveness and mercy are often conflated and considered to be synonymous. But there is a subtle distinction between the two. That distinction is evident in Mary's and Elisha's meals.

Forgiveness is a shift in feeling toward a betrayer or enemy. It is an intentional and voluntary process that begins as a victim decides to release, drop, or ignore negative emotions such as vengefulness, anger, hatred, or resentment for an offense, flaw, or mistake. It can be facilitated by putting oneself in the shoes of the betrayer and seeking an understanding of the betrayer's motivation. Though not a prerequisite, it sometimes includes the betrayer's acknowledgment of the offense or even an apology.

Examples abound: Helen stayed in the marriage with her husband after he confessed and apologized for an infidelity. Sam decided it was too difficult to keep fueling a grudge over his failure to be promoted and so forgave his boss. In their twenties, Sheila and John realized it was futile to keep blaming one of their parents for wanting a divorce.

Mary was angry with Oshea and wanted justice served. Her meetings with him at the state prison revealed his remorse and gave Mary the opportunity to get to know the person behind the crime. Her anger dissipated, and Mary found the emotional space to throw a party and meal to celebrate Oshea's release from prison and her release from a deep-seated grudge.

The Nature of Mercy

Mercy, unlike forgiveness, is not necessarily based on a change of feeling or letting go of a grudge. It is how a person—sometimes a victim, though not always—*acts* toward another: it is benevolence and compassion even amid the protestations of one's pride or ego. It recognizes a suspicion or injustice and still responds with kindness. It is the decision not to take advantage of someone in an inferior position. It does not necessarily include an apology or the offer of forgiveness.

Examples are familiar: A judge orders a lighter sentence because of a convict's upbringing or history. Still reeling from a contentious divorce, Julie heard of her ex-mother-in-law's death and sent flowers with a sympathy card. Suspicious of seeing the same panhandler at the same intersection every day, Jim nevertheless rolled down his window and offered him some loose change.

From the perspective of justice, the king of Israel had every right to demand the death of the invading Aramean army. And so did Elisha, since he knew he was the target of their invasion. But the man of God chose a different response. He decided to feed the enemy instead of slaughtering them.

Feed the Thieves

An eighth-century Benedictine hermit chose a similar response.

One night two thieves stole the oxen that belonged to Saint Philip of Zell. In trying to escape, they got lost in the woods. At sunrise, to their great dismay, the thieves found themselves back in front of Philip's hermitage.

At that very moment, the saint emerged and quickly figured out what had happened. The confused and frightened thieves begged to be forgiven.

Philip welcomed them and let them go—but only after feeding them.[3]

The Saint and the Sultan

Saint Francis's encounter with the sultan circa September 1219 led to a similar act of mercy.

During the Fifth Crusade, while sieging the city of Damietta, Egypt, the Crusaders undertook an aggressive assault on the Muslim army that ended in a devastating Christian defeat. A brief truce ensued. During this truce, Francis and Brother Illuminato arrived in the Christian camp with the hope of negotiating peace between the Christian Crusaders and the Muslim army. The two convinced Cardinal Pelagius, the papal legate who was blocking peace negotiations, to let them cross the battle lines and engage Sultan Malik al-Kamil at his court. After what could have been as many as three weeks, the two were given safe passage to return to the Christian camp. Francis left Egypt shortly thereafter and returned to Assisi.

The fact that the two friars were allowed to remain among the Muslims for several days speaks eloquently of the sultan's hospitality and the harmony arising among the three.

Though we do not know what was discussed between the saint and the sultan, we do know the conversations' effect on the sultan. After flooding the Christian camp with the waters of the Nile and engulfing the Crusaders in mud, Sultan Malik al-Kamil

3. Esper, "The Saints Can Teach Us."

allowed the incapacitated soldiers to surrender peacefully rather than having them massacred. He sent them daily bread to eat until they could leave Egypt unharmed. The Christian Crusaders, touched by such mercy and compassion, believed that the sultan had been baptized secretly by Saint Francis. He hadn't. The sultan simply made the deliberate choice for meals of mercy over a massacre by Muslims.

Jesus' Teaching

Acting with mercy was an important theme in the teachings of Jesus. In Matthew's Gospel, note the fifth beatitude at the beginning of the Sermon on the Mount: "Blessed are the merciful, for they will receive mercy" (Matt 5:7). Mercy is also listed as one of the weightier matters of the law along with justice and faith (see 23:23).

Mercy was the topic of two incidents involving Jesus and the Pharisees. In both cases, food was the precipitating factor in the conflict.

After calling Matthew the tax collector to become his disciple, Jesus ate with tax collectors and public sinners. Knowing that meals were cultural celebrations of friendship and mutual obligation, the Pharisees asked Jesus' disciples the reason for their teacher's dining with sinners. Overhearing the question and sending the Pharisees away, Jesus quoted the Greek (Septuagint) version of Hosea 6:6: "Go and learn what this means, 'I desire mercy, not sacrifice'" (Matt 9:13).

In the second incident, it is clear that the Pharisees hadn't learned the lesson. When they saw Jesus' hungry disciples walking through a farmer's field and plucking heads of grain to eat on the Sabbath, the Pharisees noted the violation of the Sabbath law. After referring to the ancient actions of David and his companions as well as the priests in the temple, Jesus again quoted the passage from Hosea: "If you had known what this means, 'I desire mercy and not sacrifice,' you would not have condemned the guiltless" (12:7).

The Gospel of Luke portrays the depth of mercy and "defines so well the boundless quality of divine mercy."[4] The passage is worth quoting in full:

> If you love those who love you, what credit is that to you? For even sinners love those who love them. If you do good to those who do good to you, what credit is that to you? For even sinners do the same. If you lend to those from whom you hope to receive, what credit is that to you? Even sinners lend to sinners, to receive as much again. But love your enemies, do good, and lend, expecting nothing in return. Your reward will be great, and you will be children of the Most High; for he is kind to the ungrateful and the wicked. Be merciful, just as your Father is merciful. (Luke 6:32–36)

Mercy clearly moves beyond the terrain of feelings. It is the deliberate decision to choose what is best for the other even in the face of their opposition. It is unbridled care, concern, and charity toward the undeserving. It expects nothing in return. Kindness to the "ungrateful and wicked" not only witnesses to one's identity before God but also is one way a disciple can imitate God's relationship to the world. Luke takes Matthew's general and abstract statement, "Be perfect, therefore, as your heavenly Father is perfect" (Matt 5:48), and gives it greater specificity: "Be merciful, just as your Father is merciful" (Luke 6:36). In his apostolic exhortation *Rejoice and Be Glad: On the Call to Holiness in Today's World*, Pope Francis states it succinctly: "Seeing and acting with mercy: that is holiness."[5]

Growing Mercy

Is there a way to facilitate this kind of holiness? Are there spiritual practices that foster a merciful lifestyle of care, concern, and kindness for every person we encounter—even the undeserving? One

4. Patella, "The Gospel according to Luke," 1122.

5. Pope Francis, *Gaudete et Exsultate*, par. 82, 44.

practical aid is the technique that can be remembered with the acronym CPR—consider, pray, resolve.

Consider the merciful people you know

Look around and observe your family, friends, and neighbors. Who stands out as being caring and compassionate? In your opinion, who are the people who personify kindness? Perhaps you can contact them, compliment them, and find out the secret to their generous hearts.

Mitchell was instantly attracted to Cheryl's thoughtfulness and selflessness. Now married to her for more than twenty years, he still stands in utter amazement at her care and concern for others. "I don't just ask, 'What would Jesus *do* in this situation?' but I also ask, '*How* would he do it?'" she once told Mitchell. On occasion, he finds himself mulling over these two questions and responding to them.

Pray the Jesus Prayer

There is an ancient tradition, found especially in Eastern Christianity, of praying the Jesus Prayer: "Lord Jesus Christ, Son of the living God, have mercy on me, a sinner."

As part of his daily prayer, Albert prays the Jesus Prayer. As he prays it, he sometimes remembers and reminisces on the times God has responded to his sins, failures, and infidelities with care, concern, compassion, and mercy. Living with the conscious awareness of God's mercy has helped soften Albert's heart, especially toward the marginalized and those often pushed aside by the institutional church. He sometimes finds himself reflecting on a verse from the Letter of James: "For judgment will be without mercy to anyone who has shown no mercy; mercy triumphs over judgment" (Jas 2:13).

Resolve to do a random act of mercy or kindness every day

Phil befriended Jerome a few years ago. "He's the kindest person I know," Phil told Albert.

"What's his secret?"

"I once asked him, and I was surprised by his answer. He said about fifteen years ago, at the beginning of Lent, he decided that a good spiritual practice to prepare for Easter would be to do a random act of kindness every day. He told me how every morning while brushing his teeth and shaving, he would decide on a 'target person' who would be the recipient of his act. He said that he enjoyed the challenge so much that on Easter Sunday, he decided he would continue the practice. And now, for the past fifteen years or so, it's become part of his daily routine and spiritual practice. It's become second nature and a habit for him."

Jerome's daily act of kindness has inspired Phil to do the same. "Sometimes it just slips my mind, but when I remember it," Phil said, "I make a point of following through."

Seeing and acting with merciful kindness rarely comes naturally. The practice of CPR helps to train the heart muscle to expand and move beyond our wounded pride and a bruised ego. We grow in kindness and compassion even toward our betrayer or enemy. As we follow in the footsteps of Mary Johnson, Elisha, Jesus, Saint Philip of Zell, and a Muslim sultan, we reflect the image of a merciful God who invites "both good and bad" to his wedding banquet (see Matt 22:10).

Reflect

When was I the recipient of someone's compassion or mercy? How did it make me feel? When was the last time I responded to a personal affront, snub, hurt, or offense with an act of mercy? How did it make me feel? Why?

Practice

Expand the size of your heart with the practice of CPR. After a week's practice, reflect on what you have learned.

Ponder

> If your enemies are hungry, give them bread to eat;
> and if they are thirsty, give them water to drink;
> for you will heap coals of fire on their heads,
> and the LORD will reward you.

—Proverbs 25:21–22

Pray

Merciful God, help me to reflect your mercy to all whom I encounter, especially those who do not treat me the way I want to be treated. Give me penetrating eyes that never judge others by appearances. Give me sensitive ears that hear the moaning of those left behind. Give me a caring tongue that only offers encouraging words. Give me generous hands that will prepare a meal for those I consider undeserving of my attention. Give me willing feet that lead to those on the margins of society. And, above all, give me a compassionate, merciful heart like that of your Son. In Jesus' name, I pray. Amen.

Conclusion

2 Kings 13:20–21

DURING THE REIGN OF Joash, king of Israel, Elisha became sick with an unnamed illness, died, and was buried (2 Kgs 13:14, 20).

The Moabites used to invade the land of Israel every spring. During one such raid, "as a man was being buried, a marauding band was seen and the man was thrown into the grave of Elisha; as soon as the man touched the bones of Elisha, he came to life and stood on his feet" (v. 21).

This miraculous story can serve as a contemporary metaphor for us. We too can be encouraged, enlivened, and reinvigorated in our spiritual lives by discovering and remembering what the life of Elisha has left behind:

- *Destroy the farm*: The call of God brooks no rivals. We are to rid ourselves of any distraction or diversion that threatens our response to God.

- *Break from the past*: Memories and past experiences can stunt our spiritual lives. We pray for the grace of healing to live in the freedom of the children of God.

- *Face opposition boldly*: Fidelity to God will bring us into conflict with others. This opposition is the expectation, not the exception.

- *Believe in the divine economy*: God is the great Almsgiver. We acknowledge that everything is a grace, a gift, and a blessing—and we share what we have been given.

- *Persist in prayer, then trust*: God hears all our prayers. We persevere in prayer and have faith that God will respond according to the divine will.

- *Be sensitive to others*: People have unique histories and sometimes find themselves in a dilemma. We respond to them with empathetic understanding.

- *Bring the small stuff to God*: God is embedded and invested in the minutiae of our everyday life. We do not hesitate to bring even the smallest requests to God.

- *Open your eyes*: God's grace and protection always surround us. We live with the active awareness of them.

- *Feed the enemy*: Mercy reflects the living God. We offer mercy to everyone, even those who do not treat us the way we want to be treated.

These spiritual practices point directly to important themes in spiritual formation:

- The call of God.

- Healing.

- Perseverance in the face of opposition.

- Gratitude and charity.

- Prayer, petition, and intercession.

- The tension between obedience to the law and Jesus' command to love.

- Living with the awareness of God's investment in every human endeavor.

- God's ever-present grace and protection in the face of trials and tribulations.

- Mercy.

Based upon incidents in the life of an ancient prophet, these nine practices are life-giving bones that God uses to instill new spirit and creativity in the contemporary believer.

Bibliography

Alter, Robert. *The Book of Psalms: A Translation with Commentary*. New York: Norton, 2007.

Anonymous. "Forgiveness and Reconciliation: The Story of Mary Johnson and Oshea Israel in Minneapolis." *WonderingEagle* blog, March 12, 2015. https://wonderingeagle.wordpress.com/2015/03/12/forgiveness-reconciliation-the-story-of-mary-johnson-and-oshea-israel-in-minneapolis/.

———. "Prayer for Inner Healing." http://www.arlingtondiocese.org/Family-Life/Prayer-for-Inner-Healing.pdf.

———. "Wesley to Wilberforce." *Christian History Institute*. https://christianhistoryinstitute.org/magazine/article/wesley-to-wilberforce.

———. "William Wilberforce." *Christianity Today*. https://www.christianitytoday.com/history/people/activists/william-wilberforce.html.

Armour, Nancy. "Why Cubs, Indians Just Gave Us Greatest World Series Game 7 Ever." *USA Today Sports*, November 3, 2016.

"Ask the Rabbi: Naar-ish." *Ohr Somayach*. https://ohr.edu/ask_db/ask_main.php/179/Q3/.

Associated Press. "Spanish Born Friar Is Canonized by Pope." *New York Times*, September 29, 1975. https://www.nytimes.com/1975/09/29/archives/spanish-born-friar-is-canonized-by-pope.html.

Bailey, Kenneth E. *Through Peasant Eyes*. Grand Rapids: Eerdmans, 1989.

Benedict XVI (Pope). General Audience. St. Peter's Square, Wednesday, May 25, 2011. http://www.vatican.va/content/benedict-xvi/en/audiences/2011/documents/hf_ben-xvi_aud_20110525.html.

Bonaventure (Saint). *Major Life*. In *Francis of Assisi: Early Documents*, Vol. 2, *The Founder*, edited by Regis J. Armstrong, OFM Cap. et al., 525–683. New York: New City, 2000.

Bonner, David, "Forgiveness and Reconciliation: The Story of Mary Johnson and Oshea Israel in Minneapolis." https://wonderingeagle.wordpress.com/2015/03/12/forgiveness-reconciliation-the-story-of-mary-johnson-and-oshea-israel-in-minneapolis/.

Burton, William L., OFM. *Abba Isn't Daddy and Other Biblical Surprises: What Catholics Really Need to Know about Scripture Study*. Notre Dame, IN: Ave Maria, 2019.

BIBLIOGRAPHY

Catechism of the Catholic Church. 2nd ed. Washington, DC: United States Catholic Conference of Bishops, 2011.

Eckhart, Meister. *The Talks of Instruction*, #22, "How We Ought to Follow God, and about Good Ways." In *The Complete Mystical Works of Meister Eckhart*, translated by Maurice O'C. Walshe, 513–17. New York: Crossroad, 2009.

Esparza, Daniel. "The Mystical Drawings of St. John of the Cross." Aleteia, December 7, 2017. https://aleteia.org/2017/12/07/st-john-of-the-cross-drawings-collection-ascent-to-mount-carmel/.

Esper, Fr. Joseph M. "The Saints Can Teach Us How to Forgive." *Catholic Exchange*, July 6, 2020. www.catholicexchange.com/the-saints-can-teach-us-how-to-forgive.

Francis I (Pope). *Gaudete et Exsultate: On the Call to Holiness in Today's World.* Huntington, IN: Our Sunday Visitor, 2018.

———. General Audience. St. Peter's Square, May 25, 2016. https://www.vatican.va/content/francesco/en/audiences/2016/documents/papa-francesco_20160525_udienza-generale.html.

Francis of Assisi (Saint). "The Testament." In *Francis of Assisi, Early Documents*, Vol. 1, *The Saint*, edited by Regis J. Armstrong, OFM Cap. et al., 124–27. New York: New City, 1999.

Hamm, M. Dennis, SJ. "Luke." In *The Paulist Biblical Commentary*, edited by Jose Enrique Aguilar Chiu et al., 1030–104. Mahwah, NJ: Paulist, 2018.

Harter, Michael, ed. *Hearts on Fire: Praying with Jesuits.* St. Louis, MO: The Institute of Jesuit Sources, 1993.

Jamart, François, OCD. *Complete Spiritual Doctrine of St. Thérèse of Lisieux.* New York: Alba House, 1961.

The Jewish Annotated New Testament. New Revised Standard Version Bible Translation. Edited by Amy-Jill Levine and Marc Zvi Brettler. New York: Oxford University Press, 2011.

John of the Cross (Saint). *The Ascent of Mount Carmel.* In *The Collected Works of St. John of the Cross*, translated by Kieran Kavanaugh, OCD, and Otilio Rodriguez, OCD, 101–352. Washington, DC: ICS, 1991.

———. *The Sayings of Light and Love.* In *The Collected Works of St. John of the Cross*, translated by Kieran Kavanaugh, OCD, and Otilio Rodriguez, OCD, 83–97. Washington, DC: ICS, 1991.

Johnson, Mary. "Mary Johnson and Oshea Israel." https://www.theforgivenessproject.com/stories/mary-johnson-oshea-israel/.

Julian of Norwich. *Revelations of Divine Love.* Edited by Halcyon Backhouse and Rhona Pipe. London: Hodder, 2009.

Levine, Amy-Jill. *Short Stories by Jesus: The Enigmatic Parables of a Controversial Rabbi.* New York: HarperOne, 2015.

Lickerman, Alex. "How to Break Free of the Past: The Past Can't Be Changed—or Can It?" *Psychology Today*, October 27, 2013. https://www.psychologytoday.com/us/blog/happiness-in-world/201310/how-break-free-the-past.

BIBLIOGRAPHY

Martin, James, SJ. "James Martin: Finding God in All Things." *On Being with Krista Tippett*, December 1, 2016 (originally December 18, 2014), https://onbeing.org/programs/james-martin-finding-god-in-all-things-2/.

Nouwen, Henri. "God's Generosity, May 5." *Bread for the Journey*. San Francisco: HarperSanFrancisco, 1997.

O'Connor, Kathleen M. "The Book of Job." In *New Collegeville Bible Commentary*, edited by Daniel Durken, 498–527. Collegeville, MN: Liturgical, 2017.

Patella, Michael F., OSB. "The Gospel according to Luke." In *New Collegeville Bible Commentary*, edited by Daniel Durken, 1108–62. Collegeville, MN: Liturgical, 2017.

Rohr, Richard, OFM. *Eager to Love: The Alternative Way of Francis of Assisi*. Cincinnati, OH: Franciscan Media, 2014.

Rolheiser, Ronald, OMI. "Sensitivity and Suffering." June 6, 2016. https://ronrolheiser.com/sensitivity-and-suffering/#.X1n7oueSnro.

Roper, David. *Seasoned with Salt: Lessons from Elisha*. Grand Rapids: Discovery House, 2004.

Sabin, Marie Noonan. "The Gospel according to Mark." In *New Collegeville Bible Commentary*, edited by Daniel Durken, 1037–107. Collegeville, MN: Liturgical, 2017.

Schmidt, Joseph F., FSC. *Everything Is Grace: The Life and Way of Thérèse of Lisieux*. Ijamsville, MD: The Word Among Us, 2007.

Singh, Simon. *Big Bang: The Origin of the Universe*. New York: Harper, 2004.

Spata, Christopher. "7 Stephen Hawking Quotes to Make You Feel Tiny, Insignificant and a Little Freaked Out." Blog post. *Tampa Bay Times*, March 14, 2018. https://www.tampabay.com/blogs/media/2018/03/14/7-stephen-hawking-quotes-to-make-you-feel-tiny-insignificant-and-a-little-freaked-out/.

Stetson, Chuck. *Creating the Better Hour: Lessons from William Wilberforce*. Macon, GA: Stroud and Hall, 2008.

Sykes, Velma West. "Two Mothers." https://www.northiowa.org/wp-content/uploads/2018/04/POETRY-TWO-MOTHERS.pdf.

Ten Boom, Corrie. *The Hiding Place*. Grand Rapids: Chosen, 1971.

Thérèse of Lisieux (Saint). *The Story of a Soul: A New Translation*. Edited by Robert J. Edmonson, CJ. Brewster, MA: Paraclete, 2006.

Thomas of Celano. *The Remembrance of the Desire of a Soul*. In *Francis of Assisi: Early Documents*, Vol. 2, *The Founder*, edited by Regis J. Armstrong, OFM Cap. et al., 233–396. New York: New City, 2000.

Toolan, David. *At Home in the Cosmos*. Maryknoll, NY: Orbis, 2003.

Toomey, Shamus. "Dead Goat Hung from Harry Statue." *Chicago Sun-Times*, October 6, 2007.

Woodward, Kenneth L. *Making Saints: How the Catholic Church Determines Who Becomes a Saint, Who Doesn't, and Why*. New York: Simon and Schuster, 1996.

Wright, N. T. *Mark for Everyone*. The New Testament for Everyone. Louisville, KY: Westminster John Knox, 2001.

www.ingramcontent.com/pod-product-compliance
Lightning Source LLC
Chambersburg PA
CBHW021825090726
47818CB00077BA/55